THE SOUL OF PLACE

CREATIVE WRITING WORKBOOK

ideas & exercises for conjuring
the *genius loci*

THE SOUL
OF PLACE

CREATIVE WRITING WORKBOOK

ideas & exercises for conjuring
the *genius loci*

LINDA LAPPIN

TRAVELERS' TALES,
AN IMPRINT OF SOLAS HOUSE, INC.
PALO ALTO

Travelers' Tales and Solas House are trademarks of Solas House, Inc. 2320 Bowdoin Street, Palo Alto, California 94306. www.travelerstales.com

Credits and Permissions are given starting on page 228.

Art Direction: Kimberly Nelson Coombs
Cover Photograph: Kimberly Nelson Coombs, farm in Pescadero, California.
Interior Design: Melanie Haage
Interior Photographs: © Linda Lappin, pages 4, 10, 87, 177, 203; © Sergio Baldassarre, page 64; © Arthur Skinner, pages 120, 146
Page Layout: Howie Severson, using the fonts Centaur and California Titling
Production Director: Susan Brady

Library of Congress Cataloging-in-Publication Data

Lappin, Linda.
  The soul of place creative writing workbook : ideas & exercises for conjuring the genius loci / Linda Lappin. -- First edition.
    pages cm
  ISBN 978-1-60952-103-5 (paperback)
  1. Creative writing--Handbooks, manuals, etc. 2. Place (Philosophy) 3. Authorship--Handbooks, manuals, etc. 4. English language--Rhetoric--Handbooks, manuals, etc. 5. Creation (Literary, artistic, etc.) 6. Travel writing--Authorship. 7. Creative nonfiction--Authorship. I. Title.
  PEI408.L319 2015
                    808'.042--dc23
                                        2015010817

First Edition
Printed in the United States of America
10 9 8 7 6 5 4 3 2 1

For the writers at Centro Pokkoli

Table of Contents

Introduction

Has it ever happened to you to fall in love with a place—your own neighborhood or an exotic locality glimpsed from a train while on vacation? There's just something in the atmosphere that has an irresistible appeal compounded of colors, scents, sounds, textures, even the taste of the air. Maybe, taking a wrong turn in a strange city, you have come upon a shady square or a house for sale that captured your imagination, but you can't really say what attracts you so much. That row of yellow bicycles parked by a crowded café with live music playing, those red geraniums on a windowsill where a sleek, black cat is snoozing and a green shutter is half-open, the chic nonchalance of people passing by with baguettes tucked under their arms? The scene triggers a fantasy in your mind: If you could just move there, something truly interesting would happen, and the story of your life would change.

Perhaps there are cherished locations in your past, the view from a mountain peak, a beach house overlooking a raging surf, or a rocking chair by a fireplace that made you feel content and at peace, or empowered and adventurous. Some places, whether indoors or outdoors, make us feel cozy and safe, inclined to daydreams. Others lift our spirits to unthinkable heights, urging us to go beyond our limits, physical or mental, There are sacred sites that can cause us to weep with remorse and humility, infuse us with joy, even make us feel immortal. Then there are other sorts of places where we become uncomfortable, on edge, oppressed, even panicky, anxious to get out of there quick—If we stay too long, who knows what bad things could happen to us there?

If you have ever had experiences similar to these, chances are that you have been touched by the power of place. This magic manifests itself in familiar as well as foreign territories, in the sublime and in the mundane, in the sacred and profane, at work in cafés, churches, temples, tombs, lighthouses, and fairgrounds. Some anthropologists suggest that our attraction to (or repulsion for) certain places derives from a deep, unconscious attunement to our environment, hearkening back to when we were all nomads, in search of suitable habitats and dependent on our instincts to lead us to water, fertile hunting grounds, or other sources of food. Back then we had a much more visceral response to our universe; we sensed where we were likely to thrive, and where not.

That instinct is not dead in us today, but we may not pay enough attention to it. Perhaps that's because much of our lives, at least in industrialized countries, is played out in what French anthropologist Marc Augé has called "nonplaces": those anonymous, deracinated spaces of shopping malls, airports, computer screens that look the same all over the world. Yet the desire to be rooted in or connected to a real place on the earth, a community, a physical world of our own, stems from a very basic human need.

The power of place isn't necessarily life enhancing. It can be threatening or devastating, pulsing with negative and positive charges that may change valence according to our personal point of view. Architects, city-planners, garden-designers, interior decorators, and before them priests, shamans, and geomancers have always known that our environment, external or internal, can be shaped to elicit certain feelings and moods, promote health or sicken us, or encourage certain behavior. They have also been aware that in modeling the landscape or constructing a building they must work with a creative force inherent in the land itself, known in the ancient classical world as the *genius loci*, usually translated as the "soul" or "spirit of place."

Most people today might define this term as the atmosphere or ambience of a locality or as the emotion or sensation that it evokes in us. To the ancient Romans, instead, it referred to an entity residing in a site and energizing it. In other words, a guardian spirit with its own personality, able to interact with human beings. A more modern conception holds that the *genius loci* is a composite of climate and landscape together with the cultural markings in a site left by its current residents and those of long ago, who shaped and cultivated its terrain, giving rise to multiple cultural forms adapted to that particular habitat. To the ancient Romans, all this was but an offshoot of the *genius loci*, whose signature is deposited in everything existing within its range of action, from bodies of water to houses, social customs, patterns of speech, artifacts, recipes, and works of art.

In their religious view, every person, place, or thing concrete—like a tree or a stone—or abstract—like love, war, or theatre—had its *genius,* an in-dwelling spark of divine nature through which that person or thing was created. The genius of an individual (for women, the *juno*) appeared at birth and accompanied the person till death. Often represented as a snake—universal symbol of time, cosmic energy, and renewal—the genius or *juno*, similar to the Egyptian *Ka*, or the Greek *daemon*, was a sort of spiritual double protecting the health, wealth, development, and success of the person to whom it belonged. The *genius loci* is specifically the genius abiding in a place.

Volcanoes, fields, villages, temples, public baths, and kitchens all had their genii, who governed and protected the site to which they were attached, determining its atmosphere and influencing the outcome of all events taking place there. If you wanted to build a house or temple in a certain spot, it was customary to seek the blessing of its *genius loci* or find a way to neutralize any negative influences that might be present there. Similar beliefs in guardian spirits of place have been recorded in such diverse cultures as Africa, Tibet, Australia, Japan, Polynesia, and the American Southwest. Today we might say that the *genius loci* is a form of intelligence operating within the environment in synergy with human beings.

Writers, poets, and artists, whose job it is to interpret and recreate reality have long been intrigued by the concepts of the *genius loci* and the power of place. Through different artistic media, they have sought ways to capture the qualities or mood of a location, to find the links between landscape and identity, to show how places can shape our personality, history, and even our fate. At the same time, many literary and artistic movements have tried to illustrate how the outer environments of human beings mirror their inner ones. Writers and artists know that whether we are looking outward or inward at our surroundings, they have a lot to reveal to us about ourselves, our present, past, and future. Consider for a moment a place that you love or hate, or that you feel emanates a power. How would you describe or define its *genius loci*? If the soul of place had a voice, how would it sound, what stories would it tell?

This book is specifically addressed to creative writers of all genres, but may also be of interest to artists in the visual and performing arts. It's a guidebook to conjuring the *genius loci* through observation and writing exercises. The material gathered here is the fruit of many years' research into what might be called "place-consciousness." It all began when I first fell in love with Italy more than thirty years ago. The passion I felt was so strong that I threw all my energies into finding a way to move there permanently, which I eventually did, struggling to make a life as a writer, teacher, and translator. The longer I stayed, the more I learned, the more I traveled, the more fascinated I became with out-of-the-way islands like Alicudi or Ventotene, mossy Etruscan ruins, Baroque sculpture gardens, Tuscan farmhouses, and other places that surfaced in my dreams and in my writing, as in my novels *The Etruscan* and *Signatures in Stone.* I slowly grew to understand how place was the prime inspiration for my work and began to investigate the many ways different locations acted upon my imagination. This research was partly theoretical, but mostly it involved traipsing about different sites and learning to listen to them, and while doing so, learning to listen to myself.

This book invites you on a journey across your personal geography to rediscover the important places in your life: from your present surroundings and your childhood home, to those magical places that may exist only in your dreams or fantasy. The writing exercises collected here will enable you to see all these locations from very new perspectives and find in them a wealth of memories, emotions, stories, voices, imagery, and inspiration. Along the way, you'll assume different identities; you'll be a country rambler, a foreign traveler, a pilgrim, a quester, a *flâneur*, a myth-maker, a homebody, a gourmet, a dreamer, and perhaps a time-traveler. You won't be alone, you'll have a guide, the *genius loci*, willing to lead you to those secret sites where a well-spring of creativity lies dormant, waiting to be tapped.

A Preliminary Exercise

Gazing at green hills and golden wheat fields from the ramparts of an old Etruscan town, D.H. Lawrence remarked that the view not only was beautiful, but had *meaning*. This English writer, often considered the founder of the modern novel, was a keen believer in the soul of place and thought it derived from biological, chemical, and cosmic influences operating in a site, affecting the psychology and behavior of individual human beings and entire populations living there. In Lawrence's view, our well-being and creativity depend on the life force manifested in our habitat, but centuries of technical progress have separated us from that force and shattered our wholeness, resulting in the aridity of modern life. One theme of Lawrence's fiction is the sacred link between identity and place and the devastation that follows when that link is broken, contaminated, or exploited for economic gain, as happens in his masterpiece, *Lady Chatterley's Lover*. Still, he believed it is possible to reconnect to that power and absorb it into ourselves, if we can just find our spot on the planet. Much of Lawrence's writing career, which he once defined as a savage pilgrimage, was a search for the fountainhead of the life force: Italy and New Mexico were among the places where he found it.

Are there places that give you a sense of wholeness and empowerment, or where you feel really *you?* Others where you feel depleted, sad, or anonymous? Make a list for both categories, then choose one from each category to work with. Reflect on the essential qualities of each place and the origins of those qualities, then write a short text of 200 words for each place you have chosen. Describe the atmosphere, narrate an episode that happened there, describe your feelings, or simply make a list of impressions, people, or things you associate with it. Put your writing aside for a few days, and if possible, revisit the sites you described, then go back and re-read what you wrote. Have you learned something new about yourself?

CHAPTER 1

Reading the Landscape

I n his poem, "A Lost Tradition," the Irish poet John Montague writes: "The whole landscape a manuscript/We had lost the skill to read." In those lines, the search for an identity connected to the territory, traditions, and language of Ireland is very specific, yet the imaginations of many writers today from all over the world will resonate with Montague's central trope: the metaphor equating landscape with text. Evoking shards of language and imagery buried in the land, Montague invites us to turn our eyes upon our surroundings, to interpret the signs scattered upon them, and unravel the stories woven into them across time.

Architects, site-specific artists, garden designers, and literary critics sometimes speak of "landscape narratives" to describe story-telling patterns and strategies present in both natural and artificial environments. Theme parks, ruins, and monumental cemeteries are obvious examples of sites where we find stories embedded, but narratives are also to be found in

1

any landscape, road, or cityscape unrolling before our eyes if we know how to look and what to look for. Learning to read our environment and translate it into stories and imagery involves heightening our attention, honing our powers of observation, and training ourselves to see patterns and to make connections between topographical features, human activities, ourselves and our inner ecologies that may appear at first glance unrelated. We need to get the bigger picture and then see ourselves in it, as the Romantic poets did, to see that we, too, are a sign upon it.

Writing Exercise: Reading the Landscape

Start by observing your surroundings: the land, sky, clouds. Note first the larger features (mountains, bodies of water, plant life, buildings) that define the limits of the space. Observe the qualities of light and climate. How do roads, buildings, and other forms of human intervention upon the environment harmonize (or disharmonize) with the climate and the lie of the land? How do local building materials (bricks, stones, wood, concrete, steel) reflect the natural setting? How might the natural resources and climatic conditions you note (timber, water, stone, earth, sunlight, rain) affect the livelihood of the place, from what you can see? How might natural features have been an asset or an obstacle to the first human beings who settled in this place? Locate north, south, east, west. Where do you stand on the compass? Where are you physically and metaphorically in this place?

Look closer to see if you can detect any recent or older damage done by fire, flooding, erosion, extreme weather conditions, or by acts of human negligence or violence. What scars or stories leap to your eye? Focus a moment on sounds, natural or artificial, and smells. If you are standing outdoors, how does the air feel around your body, your head, and on your face? How might the sum of all these things be reflected in the character of the place and, if it is inhabited, of the people who live there? Can you feel its influence on yourself in the moment you are observing it? If it's a place you've lived for a while, can you feel its influence on your personal or family history? Perhaps you see a road leading to you or away from you, or a body of water or railway track serving as a barrier or link. In what way are you part of this landscape? In what way are you separate from it? Jot down impressions randomly in a notebook as you observe the panorama.

Patterns and Textures

Study the landscape or cityscape before you as if it were an abstract design that you wish to draw or paint. Do any visual patterns emerge? Were those patterns determined by nature, by human intervention, or by the interaction of the two? Do specific geometrical shapes dominate the landscape or cityscape you are observing? Do you find a grid of city blocks, a checkerboard of fields, a cubist clutter of rectangles and domes, as Rome appears from the Janiculum Hill? Do contours of hills or dunes, winding streambeds, networks of hedgerows, or gashes of ravines plot out more organic divisions of space? Do you note examples of symmetry or repetition in the layout of buildings, roads, parks, or other spaces or features? The regular placement of telephone poles or street lamps along an urban street or trees along a country road gives a sense of rhythm to

the landscape. Can you see spiraling mountain roads, meandering rivers, labyrinthine streets? Or does a wide esplanade or avenue sweep your attention toward a central monument, square, natural feature, or building? How do swashes and streaks of color contribute to the patterns you see? If you have had the opportunity to view the place at another time of day or year, how do the diurnal or seasonal cycles affect the patterns you see? What is the largest thing you can see? The smallest? How are they connected? What looks dead? What looks most alive? Are there people in the landscape? What are they doing? Focus on faces, clothing, movement, mass, groups, or single individuals who stand out against the rest.

Now attune your eye to the textures overlaying the patterns, emerging through the combined effects of shadow, sunlight, artificial light, mist, fog, clouds, or wind upon vegetation, bodies of water, and on the ground, as well as on walls, windows, streets. Note the patterns created by the movement of traffic or other vehicles, people, lights, birds, squirrels, or other animals, vegetation, or shadows. The sounds and smells layered upon the landscape will also form patterns and rich textures of their own. Reflect a moment on how this landscape might be experienced by a blind or deaf person. What impressions would dominate their sensations of the place?

Cultures around the world make distinctions between the temporal and timeless, private and public, sacred and profane, although it may be argued that there are some cultures in which these concepts cannot be neatly disentangled. In the landscape or cityscape you are examining, are there specific localities, areas, or structures set aside for these concerns? Where are they situated in the overall pattern? What is their relationship to the whole? What is your place in all this? Sketch or draw the patterns you have noted. It isn't necessary to be artistic or skilled at drawing. Later these simple sketches will come in handy when you gather your ideas before writing.

Story Seeds

Something you didn't expect to notice will surely have seized your curiosity: a road you never knew existed; construction going on; a lower water level in a lake you used to swim in; a church or building you never noticed before; an abandoned farmhouse. Something will show signs of conflict, decay, or transformation. Every house or building encloses multiple stories. Every road or pathway is a narrative in which you may be a participant or observer. Note down anything that attracts your interest as the seed of future stories or as a subject for further investigation. Perhaps a memory has been stirred.

Writing Exercise: Transcribe Your Impressions

What color is the light? Is it filtered through leaves, columns of dust or a thick bank of thunderclouds? Does it refract off asphalt, standing water, steel, or glass? What are the houses, roofs, walls, and roads actually made of? How does the air smell and feel? How does the water taste? Italian fishermen can tell the direction of the wind even with their eyes closed by sensing its effect on their skin, by tasting it, and by the whirring it produces in their ears. Have you ever tried to taste the air, the sunshine, the rain, the wind, or the darkness? How does the ground feel under your feet? The air or water around your body? How does your skin register heat or cold? How do you feel inside your clothes (or without them) in this unique place? Take as many notes as you can dedicated to all the senses. Visual detail will probably dominate, so make a special effort to include taste, touch, hearing, and smell. Make a list or catalogue of all the impressions you have gathered, either while actually observing a place or evoking it in memory. Fill your notebook with these sensory details conveying what it's like to be immersed in that particular environment.

Working with Images

Now when you sit down to your writing desk, laptop, or tablet, translate this data into images. Writers recreate the world or invent new ones through the use of concrete language:

descriptions grounded in information drawn from all the senses: sight, hearing, smell, taste, touch. An image is a small unit of descriptive language that encodes a piece of sensory input. Although the word "image" also means "picture," when speaking of imagery in literature, we refer to all the senses. Word pictures may be visual as well as olfactory (smell), auditory (hearing), tactile (touch), gustatory (taste). Well-crafted descriptions rich with sense detail allow us to convey an impression directly rather than only *telling* about it. Through concrete imagery we may transmit sensations and feelings to the reader. We can construct a reality and bring it to life in the reader's mind.

Stripped to their essentials, images are generally composed of at least two elements:

❖ A noun and an adjective or other modifier, such as a gerund, past participle, or prepositional phrase. Example: *green shoes, punishing wind, frost-baked field, chariots of fire*

❖ A noun and a verb. Example: *the moon dwindled, the wind howled*

❖ Two nouns connected by an analogy. Example: *legs like scissors, eyes like slits*

Images can be descriptive or symbolic. Descriptive images do just what they say: describe something perceptible to our senses. Examples: *a blue mountain, a crumbling red barn, a rotten lemon, an eerie melody of swelling sound, the singed skins of oranges, the tang of wine.*

Symbolic images reach further beyond mere description and literal meaning, functioning on more than one level. They can create a link between the tangible world and inner processes or intangible things. Examples: *cloudy thoughts, a festering mind, a brooding sea.* Symbolism can endow any noun with the metaphorical power to stand for something else or point to greater meanings.

Writing Exercise: Images

Go back to the previous list or make a new one based on the environment where you actually find yourself *now.* For each sense, write two compact images. Experiment with the different forms given above.

Writing Exercise: Become an Eyeball

Landscapes have inspired some of the greatest descriptive writing in English, from William Wordsworth and Percy Bysshe Shelley to Elizabeth Bishop, Seamus Heaney, Gary Snyder, and Charles Wright. As you review the notes you have taken for the previous exercise, also consider the interchange between yourself and the landscape. "I am not alone and unacknowledged," claimed Ralph Waldo Emerson, speaking of the fields and woods where he liked to wander. "They nod to me and I to them."[1] Lawrence Durrell has also described the eerie sensation of being "watched" by a landscape.

Using all material gathered in the previous exercises, write a 200-word description in which you are a mere neutral, invisible observer, or, as Emerson once suggested, a *transparent eyeball,* viewing the scene.

Or imagine you are being watched by the landscape.

Try to work with images as described above.

See also: "Word Painting" in this chapter.

Follow Up: A Little Research

From your primary observations of the landscape, next consider the cultural markers stratified upon it: history, myth, architecture, art. Later, research, or simply reflect on, the names of localities, roads, bodies of water, streets, or other place names. Do any seem to entwine history and myth? Investigate any old maps, postcards, photographs, magazine illustrations, songs, newspaper accounts, letters, or other textual descriptions. Compare them with your findings about the place. What changes have occurred over the years?

Writing Exercise: Time Exposure

Choose a place near your home, school, workplace, or university to study over an extended period of time: twenty-four hours, a week, a month, a season, a year. It may be a busy square, a lonely road, an expanse of countryside, an urban neighborhood, a street café, a tree, the view from your window, even a parking lot. Notice how rhythms of change—hourly, diurnal, nocturnal, seasonal—affect the place. What specific details signal change? How does the place affect your thoughts and feelings? Keep a detailed journal of your impressions and the events taking place there. You will notice how your capacity to see and sense the place will deepen over time.

Place Names

Once you start investigating a territory, you'll run into some curious place names. I have a penchant for unusual street names, which I jot down in my journal. When possible, I try to photograph street signs. Here's one from Paris that I hung over my desk, Impasse des Deux Anges—which translates as two angel impasse (reminding me of Shakespeare's sonnet 144) and this one in a park in Rome right across the street from my apartment, where a broken-down old bus was transformed into a pub: Piazza on the Road, which needs no translation.

Years ago in Rome, in an antique bookshop near the Pantheon, I found a book, bound in red leather, thick as a phone directory, listing all the street names in the oldest part of the historic center and explaining their meaning and derivation. The man who ran the shop let me leaf through it for a few minutes, and as I did, I got the idea that this book could be used as a sort of aid to divination, like the tarot or the *I Ching*, and I thought that would be an interesting idea for a short story. I couldn't afford to buy it, and when I returned to the shop a few weeks later and asked to see it again, I was told that no such book had ever been sold in that shop. So my story never got written, but I still think about it from time to time.

> Name, though it seem a superficial and outward matter, yet it carrieth much impression and enchantment.
>
> — *Francis Bacon*

Place names are often messages from the past, handed down from previous generations. The poetry, history, and as Francis Bacon suggests, magic of places are often enclosed in their names. They are clues to the *genius loci*. In many parts of the world today, the preserving of place names is seen as vital to the maintaining of community heritage and even as a right protected by law.

Names are not merely words, but social practices establishing identity within a value system.[2] Place names allow us to differentiate and mark out what would otherwise be blank, undetermined, and unknowable space. In some Native American cultures, names are sacred words that cannot be disclosed without causing harm to the bearer. It is also believed that an individual "becomes" his or her name over time, which suggests that names have the power to shape and mold character and destiny. William Least Heat-Moon claims that places, too, come to take on aspects of their names, as long as they are linked to "something genuine"[3] from the outset. That something *genuine* is none other than the *genius loci*: both words "genuine" and "genius" have a common origin in the Latin "*genuinus*."

11

So what's in a name and who are the namers? By what means do places acquire names? Names encapsulate the namers' experience and their organizing of the world. Names may be descriptive, metaphorical, commemorative, dissimulating, ironic, or deprecating. They may encode features of landscape, threats, omens or warnings, ideologies, myths, desires, superstitions, euphemisms, or fragmentary memories of remote history or religion. Names can also express a form of wish-fulfillment, for example, when we give a desert road a name evoking water or trees, or try to enhance the glamor of a modest town by naming it after some great cultural capital, hoping that a little of the original charisma will rub off.

Here are some place names I have collected over the years, not far from my home in Italy. From the translations, it is easy to see that each name holds the germ of multiple stories, hinting at vaster regions of meaning.

- Piazza della Morte—Death Plaza, former seat of executions
- Piazza delle Erbe—Herb Plaza, site of a major vegetable market
- Vicolo del Macel Gattesco—Cat Butcher Alley
- Soriano from Soranus, the Roman wolf-god
- Vicolo Stretto—Narrow Alley
- Vicolo Baciadonne—Kiss Women Alley
- Vicolo dei Coltelli—Street of the Knives
- La Porta della Vergogna—The Door of Shame

- ❖ Via di Femmina Morta—Street of the Dead Female
- ❖ Via di Avio Secco—Dry Ancestor Road
- ❖ Via della Banditella—Bandit Girl Road
- ❖ Camera dei Ladri—Thieves' Chamber
- ❖ Castiglion che Dio Sol Sa—Castle That Only God Knows About
- ❖ Campo di Carne—Field of Flesh, former battlefield
- ❖ Vicolo del Mago—Magician's Alley
- ❖ And one from Greece: Odos Oneiron—Dream Street

Are there any unusual place names connected to the spaces you are investigating? Start your own list. What stories or images do they suggest to you? Take three place names and write a short text of 50 words explaining the names any way you choose.

Find a place with an unusual name and use it as the setting of a story. Or write a short essay on how it got its name, either based on research or on your imagination.

Suggested Reading

Annie Dillard, *Pilgrim at Tinker Creek*
Ralph Waldo Emerson, "Nature"
Gary Snyder, *Mountains and Rivers Without End*
Henry David Thoreau, *Walden*
Charles Wright, *Appalachia*

See also: "Making a Deep Map" in this book

Walking and Writing

What is a landscape if not a set of spaces and places linked by pathways and stories? What better way to read the landscape than by walking through it? Deep mappers and performance artists Mike Pearson and Michael Shanks affirm: The act of walking is like making a story.[4] For many poets and novelists, walking and writing are indeed intuitively interrelated activities. The act of walking gives us the leisure to commune with our thoughts as we are propelled through our environment. After all, there's no better way to see the world than by boot, quipped Bruce Chatwin (1940–1989), eminent traveler and literary travel writer. Victorian writer John Ruskin (1819–1900) would have agreed. He thought that the faster means of rail transportation of his era did not allow people enough time to appreciate the scenery. Many writers, from Thomas Traherne to Thomas Mann, have extolled walking as a way of loosening up their brains while remaining in contact with their surroundings. Thus was it for Virginia Woolf (1882–1941), who mulled over sentences and gleaned cameo portraits from passersby as she loped across the downs or "haunted" the streets of Bloomsbury. French philosopher Jean Jacques Rousseau (1712–1778) claimed that his mind could work only when his legs were busy, while William Wordsworth composed poetry

> I love a public road.
> —*William Wordsworth*

as he walked up and down outside his home, trying out new lines, "booing about," spooking his neighbors. His most ambitious work, his autobiography in verse, *The Prelude*, completed in 1805, contains memorable passages describing hikes in the countryside of his youth, over the Alps, and rambles through the streets of Paris and London; his greatest single poem, "Tintern Abbey" (1798), celebrating the restorative power of natural forms and the cosmic energy suffusing nature, was written on a walking tour with his sister Dorothy, herself an inveterate walker, who thought nothing of walking home ten miles alone at night across the countryside after a visit to the nearest neighbors. Writer Thomas De Quincey calculated that Wordsworth must have covered up to 180,000 miles in his lifetime, and believed this probably explained the even-tempered and cheerful disposition for which this great English poet was universally renowned.

"Walking" is the title of an essay by Henry David Thoreau (1817–1862) in which he famously remarked that two or three hours of walking would carry him to as strange a country as he ever expected to see. "Walking" is also the title of an essay by contemporary Native American writer Linda Hogan that takes the life cycle of a sunflower encountered during her daily walks near her home as a symbol for the great processes of nature and change in which we too are a part. The first section of her essay follows the sprouting, growth, flowering, and death of a single plant over a period of time as she witnessed its unfolding on her daily rambles.

Aside from focusing our attention on objects and phenomena encountered along the roadside, we can also focus our attention on the sensations we feel while walking. Here are two ideas:

Writing Exercise: Walking and Writing

I. **What are you walking *on*?** Whether you have set out on a pilgrimage, a quest, or just a stroll around the neighborhood, describe the sensation of your feet (bare, wearing sneakers/boots/sandals or high heels) as they touch down and lift up from any of the following surfaces:

- grass
- concrete
- sand
- dirt
- gravel
- broken glass
- granite
- wooden floors
- pine needles
- rose or jasmine petals
- moss
- cold marble
- hot, sticky asphalt
- snow
- ice
- mud
- a wet floor

❖ stairs

❖ a steep track

❖ a slippery descent

❖ a flat road

❖ thick fur

❖ grapes

❖ swampland

❖ water

❖ rubber

❖ insects, rats, or snakes

❖ fire

In your description, include smells and other sensations, such as the sound your feet make, and a description of the tracks you leave, if any.

2. **What are you walking *through*?** Describe the sensation of your feet, legs, and body as you walk through:

❖ tall grass

❖ thick trees

❖ puddles

❖ running water

❖ darkness

❖ mist or fog

- a gentle breeze
- a gusty wind
- a drizzle
- a downpour
- pelting snow
- crowds
- smoke
- flames
- traffic in motion
- a flock of sheep
- halted traffic
- mint or any other wild herb
- shadows
- brambles
- a mine field
- a tunnel
- a sewer

Describe the sensations you feel: the air around your body, on your face, lips, eyelids, in your ears, on your head, in your hair, as well as your clothes: wet, sticky, sweaty, stiff.

Use one of the above as inspiration for a poem or short narrative.

Suggested Reading

Linda Hogan, "Walking"
Gary Snyder, *The Practice of the Wild*
Henry David Thoreau, "Walking"

～

Water

Sometimes we may move through our environment not by walking but by swimming, splashing through a stream, or fighting mighty currents in a river or the ocean. Recollect the sensual experience of being immersed and moving through water. Describe the water's temperature, transparency, color, odor, consistency, and/or taste. How does it feel in your eyes, for example?

Perhaps you weren't in the water but on it. Recall a trip by boat, ferry, or canoe that took you through an exciting landscape. What does the shore look like when you contemplate it from a body of water? What mysterious lives swim or float beneath you?

Write a short text of 100 words.

∽

Deep Maps

"Deep map" is a term coined by Native American writer William Least Heat-Moon in his extraordinary book of travel essays, *PrairyErth*. After publishing a very successful "horizontal" travel book entitled *Blue Highways*, a restless, rootless ramble across America, Heat-Moon decided to take a "vertical trip" for his new project, heeding a suggestion from N. Scott Momaday in *The Way to Rainy Mountain*: to surrender himself to a particular landscape, examining it from all perspectives, wandering across it and wondering about it. [5]

In *PrairyErth*, Heat-Moon's chosen landscape is a circumscribed piece of grassland set dead center of the continental USA, Roniger Hill, from which radiates a territory of 778 square miles known as Chase County. At first glance, this place appears to be a blank in the greater void of Kansas where nothing much happens, a lonely place of transit successively abandoned by tribal peoples, settlers, speculators, and modern residents. But by the time the author has finished tracing his deep map, Chase County is revealed to be a densely woven texture of epic narratives entwining tragedy, comedy, myth, legend, and apocalypse, dating back long before the days of King Tut.

To create his topographical word map, Heat-Moon began by first obtaining twenty-five extremely detailed U.S. Geological Survey maps covering Chase County to the measure of an inch and a half to the mile, which he laid out on his living room floor and studied by walking across them. As he traversed the maps, he found they resembled a grid, like the ones used by archaeologists to map out excavations. The metaphor fit: Wasn't he also digging for "shards"? He then proceeded to test the grid against the territory, hiking across Chase County section by section "in quest of the land and what informs it,"[6] challenging the actual form of the grid itself, with its prisonlike grille of ninety-degree angles, to lead him toward his own darker, and more mysterious connection to the land.

After eight years of research and six years of writing, his end product is a vertical descent through recent and remote history into geological time. *PrairyErth* weaves together the discourses of natural history, local history, and folklore, oral testimony by local residents and scientific studies, autobiography, sociology, anthropology, archaeology, ecology. Readers become acquainted with possums, skunks, bison, coyotes, and varieties of prairie grasses; roads languishing beneath sediment and scrub, bottomlands and subterranean mountains millions of years old; burial mounds, log schoolhouses, courthouses, jails; and with the lives and legends of those hardy settlers and modern-day residents who chose to live in a place where the air is so fresh, it seems as if no one has ever used it before,[7] braving attacks by tornados and by the other apocalyptic horsemen of the prairie: Fire, Flood, and Drought. Heat-Moon's narrative of his own past memories and current response to the place mingles with the multiple voices of the prairie and with intertextual references: Tibetan sky gods, ancient Roman roads, Japanese texts, Dante's *Inferno*, and the Book of Revelation all find affinities in the heart of Kansas, entwined with the stories of native peoples who lived there six thousand years ago. Ultimately, he discovers while rambling in a half somnolent state that his real bond to the land lies deep beneath the surface, perceptible only to the non-rational mind. Facts will only carry us so far, he concludes; the only way to really know a place is to dream it.[8]

Heat-Moon's deep map resembles Bernard Anson's Map of Imagination, which we might define as a personal cognitive model of a territory that attempts to encompass all historical, spiritual, mythic, and personal data regarding that territory, layered across time. Working with the Map of Imagination brings people, stories, landscape and history into alignment. For Anson, who combines the practices of green tourism, storytelling performance art, and research into the *genius loci*,[9] the wars and peregrinations, rituals and cultural achievements enacted upon a territory *are* a manifestation of its *genius loci*, which continues to thrive and to act upon the lives and particularly upon the subconscious of its inhabitants through the centuries. By rediscovering and most especially by retelling the stories embedded in a landscape, we can better understand the ties that bind us to a place and how place itself shapes our identities. Anson describes the process of making the map:

> I proceeded without historic or geographic logic, but instead by a process of surfacing imagery.
>
> I traced epic lines, migrations, quests, pilgrimages, crusades, diasporas...
>
> I marked breaches to the underworld, oracles of the dead, sacred groves, sculpture gardens, theatres of war and Ideal Cities.
>
> I marked purgatories, infernos, and paradises.

I made blobs for warps of attrition and for *genius loci*

Thus sites of imagination surfaced from the rotating table, and slid off like great ships of light and spirit.

"You know what this is?" I cried at one point, "This is a Map of Imagination![10]

A deep map, then, is a sample swatch of the multiple manifestations of the *genius loci*. The deep map configures narratives. It is a matrix of intertextual storytelling, charting our movements through the landscape or cityscape, tracing the pathways of our habits and rituals, depositing our experiences over time in its folds, intersecting at every turn the mesh of lives and stories that have preceded us. Since the publication of *PrairyErth* in 1991, "deep map" has become a term also used by contemporary geographers and conceptual artists to refer to a sample swath in any form—textual, visual, or performance—illustrating the layers of natural, cultural, and personal history stratified upon any given geographical spot. In its meanders circulate the spirits of place.

Writing Exercise: Make a Deep Map

Although this exercise works well in both rural and urban contexts, for a first attempt I suggest trying it out in a setting where you will feel closer to nature.

Choose a rural territory, or one deeply immersed in a natural setting—a stretch of coast, or even a city park—with the intention of investigating all its byways and obscure corners. Begin by fixing the boundaries of the space you wish to study and then explore it on foot, using all your senses within those boundaries. Sketch a map of the place, or obtain one, to use as a support for your notes and drawings. Try out different routes, pathways, perspectives. Heat-Moon calls this closely focused examination of the territory "testing the grid."

Visit your chosen site at different times of day in different conditions of weather. Taste the atmosphere. Investigate its topology. Is there a particular landscape feature that attracts you, like a pond or an abandoned building? If there are roads or railways, where do they lead? Learn the local names of trees and plants, if you don't know them, and try to find out why they are important to that particular place. Observe other lives unfolding there: animals, birds, insects, people. Are there fishermen, joggers, Sunday strollers, mushroom hunters, or squatters? Notice what has been left behind in the aftermath of weather events or human occupation, fallen trees, candy wrappers, traces of recent campfires, or dead vehicles overgrown with kudzu. Who might go there at night?

Observe your personal response to all this. Take notes, pictures, videos of what you find there. Although you could limit your observation period to a single visit, deep maps take time to assemble. The more time you spend actually exploring, the richer your map will be. In between your visits, research place names, local history, local natural history, folklore, gossip, superstitions related to the place. Match your research findings with what you actually find on site. Interview residents or other walkers you meet there or local experts on its history, flora, and fauna. How does your own story weave into the territory as you proceed? How does the outer environment mirror your emotions or state of mind as you go along? Assemble your materials to build a text or multimedia project.

One way to organize your material could be to divide it into units of measure, which may be "miles," "blocks," or even "paces," and structure your text by means of your unit, i.e. you might dedicate a line/stanza/paragraph/chapter for each unit/ block/mile. Another organizing strategy is the thematic approach, selecting broad categories of themes like "water," "fire," "road stops," "woodpeckers," "danger," or whatever appeals.

Deep mapping will provide you with a wealth of information about an environment that you can transform into vivid settings in your writing. My first novel, *The Etruscan*, is a sort of deep map of Tuscia, the area north of Rome, where I love to go traipsing through vineyards and poking into Etruscan ruins. In writing my novel, I wove into the story many strands that I picked up while exploring: images of old houses and towers, animal and plant lore, superstitions, peasant traditions, even recipes that are all part of the local color and give the book a detailed, true-to-life background in contrast to the plot that is based on fairy-tale patterns.

Keep in mind that the deep map is a versatile project that can take any genre, and may be contained in a single work or spawn a series of books. You can deep map any environment, including interiors, physical or mental. May Sarton's best-selling diaries *Plant Dreaming Deep* and *Journal of a Solitude* can be read as a deep map to the poet's life, house, and garden in Nelson, New Hampshire as she worked through depression and creative blocks.

Further Suggestions:

See the exercise "Discovering the Soul of Place of Your Neighborhood" in Chapter Two for ideas in city or town environments.

Suggested Reading

André Breton, *Nadja*
Betty Cooper, *Mapping Manhattan*
William Least Heat-Moon, *PrairyErth* and *Blue Highways*
Mike Pearson and Michael Shanks, *Theatre/Archaeology*

~

Writing the Passion:
Our Emotional Response to the Power of Place

Doing the first exercise in this chapter, "Reading the Landscape," will have sharpened your senses and widened your focus, allowing you to get a very detailed impression of the place you were observing. In the "Walking and Writing" exercises, you became a character moving through the landscape, and with the "Deep Map" exercise, you began to piece together the many layers of natural and cultural information inscribed in your environment. All this will serve as a prelude to understanding your personal response to place and setting, which is essentially an emotional response blended with physical sensation.

In the West, our emotional response to landscapes both real and imagined has largely been influenced by the aesthetic beliefs informing the Romantic movement, which drew inspiration from even earlier schools of philosophy investigating the restorative role of nature in human life. Our perception of nature and our appreciation of its beauty have greatly been determined by the Romantic concepts of the *beautiful* and the *sublime.*

Nowadays, the words "beautiful" and "sublime" are sometimes used almost as synonyms, with the latter referring to something that is beautiful to an extreme degree, capable of arousing in us ecstasy or overwhelming pleasure. Music, food, drugs, majestic landscapes, passionate sex, art, and sunrises are often described as sublime. The Romantic poets had a different approach. In their eyes, the pleasure of the sublime was always tinged with fear or the threat of annihilation, because there can be no pleasure without death. Immersion in nature with all its dangers was for them the prime source of sublime experience.

What do these words mean to you? Take a few minutes to think about it, then write your own definition for "beautiful" and "sublime," adding examples of things or experiences you would describe in these terms.

⌒

The Romantic Ideals of the Beautiful, *the* Sublime, *and the* Picturesque

The Romantic poets William Wordsworth (1770–1850), Samuel Taylor Coleridge (1772–1834), Percy Bysshe Shelley (1792–1822), and John Keats (1795–1821) have often been credited with the "rediscovery" of nature in English poetry. This is not to say that there were not great "nature poets" in previous periods of English literature. Shakespeare is one of the greatest nature poets of all time, as any student who has investigated the rich nature imagery of his plays and sonnets knows. What changed with the Romantics was the focus or perspective. Whereas earlier poets like Shakespeare saw natural phenomena as symbols of human emotions, states, or values, the Romantics often saw themselves as the mirror of nature, and celebrated natural objects—trees, rocks, wind, clouds, and mountains—as manifestations of a great power animating the universe and the human mind, and also as absolute values in themselves. They viewed the natural environment as a source of wisdom, inspiration, and healing and as a refuge from the artificial constructions of society. They also sought to capture rhythms and manners of natural speech in their poetry, and explored the writing of poetry as an organic process.

The literary movement known as Romanticism spanned nearly a century (roughly 1770–1870) creating a new sensitivity toward nature and the natural environment, and also toward the people who lived in closer contact with the cycles of the natural world: farmers, inhabitants of rural areas (favorite subjects of Wordsworth's poetry), fishermen and sailors, aboriginal peoples, and children. The Romantics believed that through contemplation of nature or by living in close contact with it, human beings may have access to higher states of consciousness and that these states are naturally accessible to children. In the visual arts, the Romantic aesthetic expressed itself in the new popularity of landscape painting over portraiture. Walking tours became a favorite pastime for Londoners wishing to escape the crush and pollution of their city. Wordsworth himself wrote a travel guide to the Lake District for walkers. Unschooled poets like John Claire (1793–1864), the farm laborer who wrote poetry about the countryside, also enjoyed a vogue for they incarnated Wordsworth's belief that men living in closer contact with nature would naturally be more inclined to poetry. These writers, painters, travelers, and walking tourists viewed landscape according to three main qualities celebrated by the aesthetics of the period: the beautiful, the sublime, and the picturesque.

The first two are treated in Edmund Burke's *Treatise on the Sublime and the Beautiful* (1756), which had a deep impact on the age's perception of nature and art. Burke's ideas still touch us today. Essentially, Burke claimed that human beings have two basic instincts, self-propagation and self-preservation, which provide the foundation for all human emotions and passions. The objects we perceive in our world appeal to either one or the other of these two subconscious instincts. Things that are pleasing to our senses because they possess the qualities of smoothness, softness, or harmony speak to the instinct of self-propagation and pertain to the realm of the *Beautiful*. Those that evoke fear, pain, antagonistic forces, or infinity appeal to the instinct of self-preservation and pertain to the realm of the *Sublime*. In addition to the idea of danger, the sublime embraces the idea of power: "Strength, violence, pain and terror are therefore ideas which occupy the mind together. The sublimity of wild animals is due to their power; and the power of princes is not unmixed with terror, so that we address them as 'dread majesty.'"Yet, there is pleasure in horror: "Infinity fills the mind with that sort of delightful horror which is the truest test of the sublime."[11] Burke went on to analyze why the human mind feels so drawn to that which is terrifying, empty, vast, or infinite: it actually enjoys "being conversant" with infinity, vastness, emptiness, and other terrifying objects when it may contemplate them without danger to itself. This explains why movies about apocalyptic catastrophes are so appealing.

Moreover, says Burke, *the mind may take on some of the qualities of what it perceives.* The vastness of the sea, the depth of the ocean, the power of a storm thrill us when perceived in a work of art, or from a perspective in which we are not in danger. We become part of them and they of us through this operation of the mind.

Burke identified seven attributes of the sublime:

1. obscurity (that which induces terror)

2. power

3. privation (vacuity, darkness, solitude, silence)

4. vastness (height and depth)

5. infinity (including artificial infinity)

6. succession (an endless progression of the mind beyond limits)

7. uniformity

In addition to these two categories of the beautiful and the sublime, other Romantic writers and painters later identified a third aesthetic quality that they called "the picturesque," which has been defined as neither beautiful nor sublime, but mixing the qualities of roughness, variation, irregularity, and strangeness or oddity. An entire school of picturesque painting and literary travel writing developed around these ideas. These three principles—"sublime," "beautiful," and "picturesque"— still influence our perception of our environment and provide the aesthetic framework for much memorable literary travel writing produced by Western writers. In contemporary travel writing, the penchant for the offbeat or incongruous found in the work of some very fine writers is simply a further evolution of the "picturesque."

Not all cultures share Burke's interpretation of the sublime. According to traditional Chinese aesthetics connected to the practice of Feng Shui, an art or perhaps a science that deals with the placement of buildings in a natural landscape, the view of the sea from a house perched on the edge of a cliff as in Big Sur is not attractive but repellent. The Western mind finds ancient ruins in the countryside overgrown with weeds "picturesque," and in different periods of architectural history it has been fashionable to decorate gardens and parks with fake ruins. To practitioners of Feng Shui, however, these are dangerous portents of decay with nothing appealing about them.

Japanese aesthetics, influenced by Zen and the Buddhist concepts of impermanence and the void, identifies specific qualities of the natural world that the artist must try to capture spontaneously, without effort, in a work of art, merging his identity with the void from which that manifestation springs. Evanescence and "Whatness" are two of these aesthetic categories that find no exact correspondence in Burke's theories. Still, these two qualities may express the soul of a place.

The following passage from my mystery novel, *Signatures in Stone*, plays with these three Romantic concepts as forces in the Italian landscape. Can you identify them? How do they make you feel? What do they say about the narrator?

About a hundred miles north of Rome, we turned inland to cross a marshland, then a succession of arid hills where broken bits of ancient Roman aqueducts stood stark against the twilight. Farther on, deep ravines gashed the terrain like unhealed fissures from which rose twisted masses of gray stone where ancient houses, domes, and grottoes were chiseled along the edges. Only a great turbulence from deep within the earth could have gouged out such chasms which appeared before us with hardly any warning as we rolled along. Flat meadows fell away into gorges where the road plunged, then laboriously wound up again. Thorny bushes scraped the sides of the car in narrow spots; jutting rocks thumped against the belly of the vehicle, causing Nigel great concern for his axel. God knows what would have happened if the car had broken down out there in the middle of nowhere. We might have been devoured by wolves, or by the ferocious white sheepdogs that pounced out of the brush to run alongside the car until their legs gave out, barking their heads off till we rounded the next curve.

Sometimes on a promontory we saw a cluster of houses, now all dark, or an isolated farmhouse with a yellow glimmer at the window or a curl of smoke above the chimney; sometimes a dilapidated church or hermitage nestled in a crevice along a cliff. The landscape was full of signatures, signs, and hidden meanings, I felt. An entire manuscript was displayed before my eyes, inviting me to decipher its alphabets, offering inspiration for the new novel I had come to Italy to write at Nigel's forceful insistence.

Suggested Reading

On the sublime:
Elizabeth Bishop, "The End of Travel"
Percy Bysshe Shelley, "Mont Blanc"
William Wordsworth, "Tintern Abbey"

Look for poems, passages of fiction, memoirs, essays, or literary travel writing that contain detailed place descriptions. Notice if the elements of the sublime, beautiful, and picturesque are present, and which ones appeal to you most

Writing Exercises Inspired by the Romantics

Make three columns on a piece of paper for beautiful, sublime, and picturesque. If "picturesque" seems too tame for you, substitute it with "weird" or "strange." Without pausing to think too deeply, write down ten things—people, places, objects, experiences—for each column. Then choose three and write a passage of 50 words for each one.

Poetry is the spontaneous overflow of powerful feelings recollected in tranquility.

—*William Wordsworth*

A Sublime Moment

Recall a moment you have experienced, either in a natural or artificial environment, when you were touched by a powerful emotion, a great silence, a sense

of nothingness, or an overwhelming sound. Describe your surroundings and sensations using concrete imagery as explained
previously in this book. Use this as the basis for a lyric prose
piece, essay, or poem. You needn't limit yourself to experiences
in nature. One of my students wrote a very moving essay on the
sublime in which he described being in a stadium with thousands of other people during a soccer match.

A Moment in Nature Recollected in Tranquility

Recall a past moment of powerful feeling in nature and recreate
it in a poem, memoir fragment, or short fiction piece in which
one of these three modes dominates—sublime, beautiful,
picturesque.

A Moment of Danger

Have you ever found yourself in an extremely dangerous situation while alone in a natural setting? Recall the experience.
Perhaps the danger was real and objective, or only experienced
as such. Structure your text as follows:

❖ First, focus on the moment when your awareness of the
circumstances was most intense. Describe it.

❖ Next, flash back to recount how you got there.

❖ In your final phase, focus on the resolution of the situation and your release from fear.

The Seven Categories

With reference to Burke's seven categories of sublime perceptions: obscurity, power, privations, vastness, infinity, succession,

and uniformity—choose one to describe as a landscape or setting. Then craft a flash fiction story or memoir fragment taking place there.

William Wordsworth's Spots of Time

> There are in our existence spots of time,
> That with distinct pre-eminence retain
> A renovating virtue.
>
> —*William Wordsworth*

In 1798, in a moment of poetic frustration, suffering from what we might call today a form of writer's block, Wordsworth undertook a major project that some consider his masterpiece: an autobiography in verse posthumously entitled *The Prelude, or the Growth of a Poet's Mind.* Continually reworked and revised over a period of forty years, the final version published after his death runs thousands of lines in fourteen books.

Wordsworth's intention in *The Prelude* was not self-celebration of what was unusual or unique about his personality. On the contrary, he desired to stress the psychological processes of growth, perception, and intellectual and emotional development common to all human beings and therein, he believed, lay the poem's value and interest for his readers. Like much of Wordsworth's great poetry, *The Prelude* deals with the Self in nature, tracing the process through which the child's sense of oneness with the natural world splits into a keen sense of separateness from nature and from others. The poem is built around flashes of vivid memory and heightened consciousness that Wordsworth defined as "spots of time." For Wordsworth, these "spots" were sometimes linked to specific moments of joy in the natural world or other intense emotions in childhood that he later relived through memory in all their intensity, accompanied by strong physical sensation. To experience a spot of time brought him healing, redemption, and enhanced imaginative power, for the memory of these experiences, re-elaborated with the greater intellectual understanding granted by maturity, was the prime source of his poetry. Some of the more famous spots of time in the poem are related to a physical activity, like ice-skating on a pond under the stars or climbing a mountain. Still others arise from powerful emotional feelings, like guilt over stealing a rowboat, or grief for the death of his father. In *The Prelude*, Wordsworth uses these spots to plot the course of his development—spiritually, emotionally, and intellectually—over the decades of his life.

Later writers have evolved similar concepts. Virginia Woolf's "moments of being," and James Joyce's epiphanies are similar to Wordsworth's spots of time. Take some time and look back over your life. Childhood is a good place to begin, but you need not limit yourself to that period. Can you identify "spots of time," luminous, distinct moments from the past connected with being in a special outdoor setting? Choose one and begin writing freely—describing the experience itself, how it felt then, *and* the act of remembering the experience: how it feels now to recall it. Give yourself a time limit of up to 30 minutes for this exercise.

For a more demanding project, try to identify a series of spots of time related to crucial moments in your life and connect them through a narrative, either in prose or poetry.

Postcard Narratives

Art historians have noted that the pathways and panoramas of the gardens of Versailles were designed as landscape narratives to provide the visitor with a series of views or scenes, all to be savored while pausing in a particular spot and gazing from a particular perspective. The baroque landscape designers who created the great Italian gardens of the sixteenth century also intended for visitors to experience fountains or statuary from specific positions and angles along a predetermined itinerary. Travel guides written in the Romantic period often suggested "stations" from which the traveler should view natural scenery in order to fully appreciate its beauty. Those marvelous gardens and Romantic landscapes had been parceled up and pre-packaged into a series of snapshots or postcards, before the postcard was actually invented.

Flimsy, cheap, and ephemeral, postcards announce to the receiver, *I have seen this.* Like footprints, they leave a trail of where we have been, which we may then send to someone else or hide in a drawer. Autobiographical, but public, unlike a sealed letter, they may be read by anyone under whose eyes they happen to fall. Typical subject matter of picture postcards includes: historic monuments and landmarks, panoramas, quaint scenes off-the-beaten-track, close-up views, details, objects of desire, and of course, erotic, humorous, or bawdy scenes. Writers as diverse as Jacques Derrida, Annie Proulx, and Robert Olen Butler have been intrigued by the interplay of iconic image and short, revelatory personal text to be used as building blocks for longer, more complex narratives.

The *sublime, beautiful,* and *picturesque* are typical qualities immortalized in picture postcards sold as souvenirs, a custom that gained popularity over the latter half of the nineteenth century in connection with industrial feats such as the construction of the Eiffel Tower or the consolidation of the British Railways. The first postcard in the United States was printed in Chicago to celebrate the World's Fair of 1893, ushering in an era of mass production and mass communication. While often based on clichés and stereotypes, picture postcards also capture authentic aspects of the soul of place. Postcards are reflections of the Zeitgeist—the spirit of a particular time, revealing how a culture sees itself. The visual politics of vintage postcards are studied by cultural historians today to understand and reconstruct the past concerning travel, leisure, and colonial assumptions of otherness.

Like many travelers, I am a compulsive purchaser of postcards. Over the years, I have filled suitcases with views of the cities I have visited or dream of visiting, artworks in museums, ruins, portraits. Some of my favorites are Venice in the snow, the Coliseum under the full moon, cars floating in the Florence flood, and two views of a street in Warsaw, one bombed out by the war, the other rebuilt. I like to lay them out in random sequences, like Tarot cards, and guess the connections—the links, gaps, and itineraries lying in between. American novelist Robert Olen Butler had a similar compulsion. After collecting postcards for ten years, he realized he had the backbone of a short story collection, later to be published with the title, *Had a Good Time.*

S. 167   DON.CE.SAR HOTEL BY MOONLIGHT. PASS-A-GRILLE. FLORIDA

From Epistolary Novel to Postcard Narratives

One of the first novels in English, *Pamela*, by Samuel Richardson (1740), consists of letters written by the heroine to her parents describing her attempts to refuse the undesired advances of her employer. The now popular postcard story/novella/novel is a condensed derivative of that early fictional experiment. Postcard narratives may be viewed as single episodes of up to 200 words (or short enough to fit on the back of a single postcard) or as a sequence of such short texts somehow relating (or not) to the image on the front. There are specific contests for this short short/flash fiction/creative nonfiction genre—one well-known contest is sponsored by the Canadian Writers Union.

Writing Exercises for Postcard Narratives

For the following exercises, you'll need a few postcards, including vintage ones. If you can't find any at home stashed in a drawer, look for them at garage sales, on eBay, or in a friend's attic.

PUT YOURSELF IN A POSTCARD: Take a postcard and put yourself in the picture. First, describe the scene from your point of view as if you were in the picture, either in full view or hidden. Tell the story that brought you to that place or narrate what is taking place outside the picture. Sometime later, pick up the postcard again and re-read your text. What happens in the next scene? Find another postcard to continue your narrative. Consider: two postcards stuck side by side in a sequence make a narrative. Find the links between them.

CHOOSE TEN POST CARDS: Give them an order, and write a narrative of no more than 100 words per card. It need not describe a journey, but may follow any process or reflect changing moods or perspectives upon an event. Consider the gaps or transition between each image. How do you close one scene and propel the reader to the next? Send the postcards to another person who might want to continue the story and ask them to add another sequence of cards and texts to send back to you, or perhaps on to someone else. This is a fun group project.

As a variation on this exercise, invent a series of postcards with digital images to describe a place you have visited, or a specific period in your life. Each postcard text should be a maximum of 100 words.

Your task is to link each image to the text in an unusual way.

FIND FIVE VINTAGE POSTCARDS that have actually been mailed and have a message written on the back and a postmark. As you study the messages, consider that these are traces of real lives. Try to imagine the people who wrote them and the feelings and circumstances attached to each card. Why did the sender choose that particular card? Where did they get the card? Who were they writing to and why? Does the handwriting give you any clues about the sender? How do you suppose the receiver responded? Use the messages, images, and postmarks to create a character and a story for a longer piece of fiction/creative nonfiction.

STORY PROMPT: A woman, age 35, opens the mailbox to discover a postcard of an exotic place she has never heard of, addressed from a seemingly unknown person. Use these three elements, sender/receiver/message, as the basis of a story. Take it from there.

Suggested Reading

Robert Olen Butler, *Had a Good Time*
Annie Proulx, *Postcards*

～

The Art of the Travel Tweet

Some people may be surprised to find a note on Twitter in a book of creative writing exercises. There is no doubt that the textual forms favored by social networks have become and will remain standard forms of writing, and anyone who aspires to excel in the art of travel writing must master the travel tweet. Writing teacher Evan Rail compares the tweet to a haiku: short and evocative. Thanks to the compressed and concrete nature of this form of 140 characters, working with tweets is a good way to get your creativity flowing and an excellent exercise for the first day of a new writing class. Tweets will add sparkle to any travel journal.

Worldhum, a website showcasing contemporary travel writing, interviewed several well-known travel writers and editors to ask what they thought made up a good travel tweet. They concurred that good travel tweets should:

- Include text, pictures, hashtags, and links
- Use correct grammar and spelling
- Capture the atmosphere or spirit of place
- Encapsulate a narrative in 140 characters
- Be pithy and keep the focus tight
- Have a light touch and be fun, quirky, or surprising
- Offer a window on your unique experience of a place
- Be specific and direct
- Avoid being too self-referential
- Transcend limits of the personal by aiming for something larger than oneself
- Be useful to others to read by sharing resources
- Invite interaction with readers
- Avoid complaining

Some examples from my students:

Trains eat away at my time. Platforms and stations are the dirty truth of public transportation. —J.C.

Chilled champagne bottle in hand, my reality surreal. This is Paris! —J.C

Tower of Methoni at the hotel window. Solitary sentinel conversing at dawn with the full moon. —S.B.

Writing Exercise: Travel Tweets

Write five tweets describing your neighborhood, or a place you have recently visited on a trip. Look for the beautiful, sublime, picturesque, strange, or comic. Strive for a haiku effect, and include humor in at least one.

⌒

Word Painting

In previous centuries, before the invention of postcards or the preponderance of photography in our lives as the primary source of information about our world, people came to know distant places like America, the Arctic, and Africa, through engravings, paintings, and especially textual descriptions by writers who had visited those places (or perhaps only pretended to have done so). John Ruskin (1819–1900), Victorian writer and educator, author of some of his era's most important travel writings, championed the art of "word painting" for the purpose of conveying visual impressions of a place through words. Ruskin took a painterly approach to writing, and in his descriptions sought precision in rendering colors, textures, shadows, nuances, and atmospheres, many areas of perception for which we don't always have a subtle or complete vocabulary with which to notate our sensations. Some passages of Ruskin's word painting describing the movement of clouds suggest an almost cinematic technique. According to Ruskin, when we photograph or depict something by painting, drawing, or writing about it, or simply when we buy a postcard, what we are really trying to do is capture part of the beauty of the place so that we may take it home and preserve it for our future enjoyment.

Word painting techniques are used to create detailed descriptions of landscape in travel writing, as well as settings in fiction. Writers of gothic novels used similarly vivid landscape description to convey not only the physical setting but also the interior moods of characters and to foreshadow plot developments.

Study the following examples of word painting from different historical periods in literature. Are any other senses besides sight engaged? Note how each "scene" is depicted from a specific perspective or angle as if viewed by an encompassing eyeball.

Three Examples of Word Painting

> On this mound is built a rude brick campanile, of the commonest Lombardic type, which if we ascend towards evening (and there are none to hinder us, the door of its ruinous staircase swinging idly on its hinges), we may command from it one of the most notable scenes in this wide world of ours. Far as the eye can reach, a waste of wild sea moor, of a lurid ashen

grey; not like our northern moors with their jet-black pools and purple heath, but lifeless, the color of sackcloth, with the corrupted sea-water soaking through the roots of its acrid weeds, and gleaming hither and thither through its snaky channels.

—From John Ruskin, *The Stones of Venice* (1851)

The green land, with squares of leaden-dark olives planted in rows, slopes down to the railway line, which runs along the coast parallel with the ancient Via Aurelia. Beyond the railway is the flatness of the coastal strip, and the whitish emptiness of the sea's edge. It gives a great sense of nothingness, the sea down there.

—From D.H. Lawrence, *Etruscan Places* (1932)

The road to the tombs skirted a field of shriveled sunflowers, an army of nodding heads on stalks, bowed and blackened, awaiting harvest. There were no houses out this way, only wide expanses of tawny stubble, alternating with strips of freshly ploughed clay. Here and there on a hilltop, a dead oak or cypress punctuated the empty sky where hungry crows swooped low.

—From Linda Lappin, *The Etruscan* (2004)

The first passage by Ruskin emphasizes the decaying grandeur of Venice at the time of his visit. His diction, or choice of words, heightens our sense of desolation and decay: *ruinous, waste, lurid, ashen, lifeless, sackcloth, corrupt, snaky.* The second passage by Lawrence seeks to recreate the geometrical patterns in the landscape: *squares, rows, line, parallel, flatness, strip* and the emotions the overall pattern stirs in the viewer: a sense of nothingness. The third aims for a more symbolic description, linking the narrator's inner world with portents of change, maturity, decay, and danger appearing in a lonely landscape: *shriveled, bowed, blackened, awaiting harvest, dead oak, empty sky, hungry crows.*

Writing Exercise: Word Painting

Find examples of word painting in some of the books you love: fiction, nonfiction, travel. Examine the author's word choice to see how he achieves a vividness of detail. Then go back to a story, travel essay, or memoir you have already written and rewrite a passage of description using the technique of word painting. Or write a 300-word description of your current environment using this technique.

More Maps

The deep map, as we saw earlier in this chapter, takes a hands-on approach to a territory. It works best with a site we can actually explore on foot, making notes as we go. But we can also use maps as writing prompts and as organizing and structural tools for narratives. Maps, like novels or poems, are replicas of the physical world, models of the human mind, and in some traditions—diagrams of the soul. For me they have always been a source of inspiration: one of the earliest toys I remember is a jigsaw puzzle map of Europe. My favorite piece was the yellow boot of Italy—prophetic perhaps, since that country was to become my home. Maps to buried treasure, star charts, city plans, and architectural blueprints are forms familiar enough to us. But maps may appear in other guises: in the Buddhist tradition, mandalas are maps of states of consciousness; in Persia the patterns of carpet designs sometimes charted the unfolding of the cosmos or the pathways of paradisiacal gardens.

Maps needn't take a visual form and may consist of words or music. In Australia, the songlines of the aboriginal tradition investigated by Bruce Chatwin are actually word maps of a territory, transmitting both topographical knowledge necessary for human survival and sacred knowledge concerning its mythic origins and cosmic meaning. Maps may also be imprinted in the circuits of our neurons. French philosopher Gaston Bachelard has noted that we carry the map of our first environment within us as a bundle of buried reflexes developed through our earliest movements within our first home.

Some of the twentieth century's greatest novels are actually structured on maps. It is often said that to get the full enjoyment out of Joyce's *Ulysses,* you should read the book with a map of Dublin and a clock in hand. Similarly, Virginia Woolf's *Mrs. Dalloway* is, in a way, a map of London, while J.D. Salinger's *Catcher in the Rye* is of New York City. In more recent times, Thomas E. Kennedy's masterpiece, *The Copenhagen Quartet,* incorporates a map and even a guidebook to the monuments, sights, pubs, and eateries of that Nordic capital.

We all have our private maps of the neighborhoods, houses, rooms where we have lived. In those mental maps, the physical features of the place are less important than the atmosphere and our response to it, that magical connection between the soul of place and our imagination. Such maps are uniquely individual to each lover of a place. No two will be alike. Our private maps localize and identify the soul of place as it has interacted with us on an individual basis and influenced our lives.

Writing Exercise: Make a Mental Map

Choose an environment or a time-space continuum. It may be a city, town, neighborhood, landscape, house, or a period of consecutive time, such as: "the winter I lived in Florence," "the month I lived in my car," or cyclic: "The many summers I spent at my grandmother's house on the lake when I was a child." Quickly write down a list of five significant spaces in the continuum. Interpret "space" freely—it can be as small as the space inside a box or as large as the Grand Canyon.

For each space on the list, make a sub-list, using the ideas below. Your sub-list may be as long or as short (even a single item) as you wish. You could include:

❖ Objects or people related to the spaces (landscape features, furnishings, food, clothing, etc.)

❖ Sensations connected with specific places and objects

❖ Feelings and emotions connected to specific places and objects

❖ Events that happened there to you

❖ Seasonal indications, weather, relevant dates or days of the week

Now draw the map as detailed or sketchily as you wish. It doesn't matter if you're not artistic or if it doesn't correspond to geographical reality. Drawing and doodling use different brain functions than language and can help free up energies or unleash memories. Give it a try!

Connect some places with lines, showing some progression or movement as you experienced it. Interpret this freely; it need not be chronological or logical. This is your mental map. Now use this as a writing prompt.

Write a short passage of 50 words for each significant place, drawing on ideas in your list. Use the map to structure a narrative or lyric prose piece of memoir or fiction.

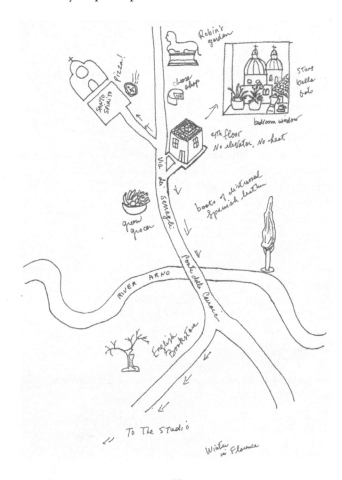

The Winter I Lived in Florence

I. *The house in Via dei Serragli*
    4th floor, no elevator, no heat
    The window on the Carmine church dome. Bells, bats, stars.
    The gas space heater, a corona of blue flame in the tin dish.
        The tainted smell of the air
    The kitchen bare white walls, pots on nails.
        A. eating spaghetti with tomato from a tube.
        D. frying liver and onions for breakfast
    The smell of chlorinated water. Boiling water to save money on
    bottled mineral water
    A borrowed typewriter on the scarred table

2. *Piazza Santo Spirito*
    The church with its naked façade
    The pizzeria on Saturday nights. Always the cheapest: a margherita
    The sad girl with a blue beret eating there alone
    Posters for Abba and The Pooh
    A cappuccino cost 80 lire!

3. *Bridge il Ponte della Carraia*
    Freezing winds sweeping down from the hills
    Buses trundling full speed
    My black wool cape flapped in the wind
    Boots of distressed Spanish leather
    Second-hand books at the English bookstore, Keats and Coleridge

4. *The studio*
    A torn wrinkled map in my pocket
    Icons and statues. Cherubs and fountains.
    The smell of resin and printers ink
    Always classical music on the radio. And the smell of fresh coffee
    brought from the bar downstairs.

5. *Robin's garden*
    Money trees and cats
    The shadow of the sphinx

⌒

Bringing It All Together: Final Projects

In this first chapter, you have been given a variety of tools, exercises, strategies, and perspectives, ranging from concrete imagery and word painting to postcard narratives and mapping techniques.

1. Select an outdoor environment, explore it, deep map it, and organize the material you have gathered in a travel essay, memoir, or narrative poem, incorporating any techniques and ideas from this first chapter. Try to express its particular soul of place and your connection to it, what it means to you, what larger ideas it allows you to discuss, what it has taught you about life and about yourself.

2. Mentally reconstruct a deep map of a landscape or neighborhood that belongs to your past, applying ideas and techniques suggested in this chapter.

3. Writing prompt: "I was the world in which I walked," wrote Wallace Stevens. Let your imagination dwell on this phrase, then write a lyric essay, poem, or travel narrative to illustrate your own experiences, while exploring the ideas in the first chapter.

4. Combine a deep map project with a postcard narrative.

5. Take a short trip to a new destination and tweet about its soul of place. Try to use concrete images from all the senses.

6. Write about a sublime experience dealing with water or fire.

7. Weave the concepts of the beautiful, sublime, and picturesque into a travel essay. Use word-painting techniques.

8. Describe being lost in the woods.

9. Write an ode to a volcano or an island.

10. Write about an extreme weather event or natural catastrophe to which you were a witness, in 350 words.

11. Write about survival in the wilderness, in the desert, or at sea.

12. Keep a nature diary about an environment near your home or workplace.

13. Write about a place in nature that makes you feel empowered or energetic.

14. Write about a place in nature that makes you depressed or afraid.

---

[1] Ralph Waldo Emerson, *Nature*, in *Complete Works* 12 Vols. Boston: Houghton-Mifflin, 1903–1904, 5, p. 288.

[2] Matthew Potteiger and Jamie Purinton, *Landscape Narratives, Ibid, p. 75–76.*

[3] William Least Heat-Moon, *PrairyErth A Deep Map*, New York: Houghton Mifflin, 1991, p. 118.

[4] Mike Pearson and Mike Shanks, *Theatre/Archaeology*, New York: Routledge, 2001, p. 138.

[5] N. Scott Momaday, *The Way to Rainy Mountain*, Santa Fe: University of New Mexico Press, 1969, p. 83

[6] Heat-Moon, op.cit., p. 10.

[7] So claims a local resident. See Heat-Moon, p. 83.

[8] Ibid. p. 105.

[9] http://www.storygardenz.com/whatis/moi

[10] Bernard Anson Silj, *Carmen Via*, The Hague: Semar, 2005, p. 128.

[11] Edmund Burke, A *Philosophical Enquiry Into the Origin of Our Idea of the Beautiful and Sublime*, London: J.J. Tournesin: 1792, p. 109.

CHAPTER 2

Places Sacred and Profane—
Pilgrims and *Flâneurs*

The Writer as Pilgrim

Traveling, writing, and storytelling have always been intricately connected. We know of the heroic journeys of exploration, scientific expeditions, or intimate pilgrimages that took place centuries ago thanks to the detailed accounts recorded by travelers. All these forms of travel have produced great works of literature but the genre of the pilgrim's narrative recounting a quest undertaken for spiritual reasons is an especially rich literary tradition that has been popular throughout the ages, from the fifteenth-century *Book of Margery Kempe*, the first autobiography in English, to the contemporary cult book and global bestseller *The Pilgrimage* by Paulo Coelho.

The term pilgrim is usually defined as a person who travels to a holy site as a devotee. The word itself derives from *per agros*, meaning "through the fields," i.e. "outside the city," suggesting a stranger, a wanderer, an outsider, someone unbound to the rhythms of the city, looking for something else in life, if only momentarily. The undertaking of pilgrimages to visit a holy site, shrine, or tomb is a universal pattern in world religion. Setting out on a quest to retrieve something or someone lost or to obtain a treasure, such as the promised land, the golden fleece, or the fountain of youth, is a universal trope in myth, legend, literature, and history. One of the world's oldest metaphors, "life as a journey, pilgrimage, or quest " can be traced back to what may be the first recorded narrative poem, the Sumerian *Epic of Gilgamesh* in which the hero's search for the Land of Utnapishtim represents a path to initiation, and the places he visited and the deeds he performed along the way symbolize states of consciousness attained in a journey towards self-knowledge.

The timeless quest narrative has tantalized the imagination of every generation. Literary works as diverse as *The Odyssey, Amor and Psyche, Heart of Darkness, The Rime of the Ancient Mariner, To the Lighthouse, On the Road, Mutant Message from Down Under,* and *Harry Potter and the Deathly Hallows* all share its basic threefold structure of DESIRE-CONFLICT-BREAKTHROUGH. The quest narrative is not only the foundation of fairy tales and myths, but provides the underpinnings for many works of fiction, creative nonfiction, and memoirs, especially those dealing with illness or addiction and recovery.

Sacred Space

Pilgrims set out on their quests seeking spiritual rewards: transformation, penitence, healing, or inner enrichment by traveling to or through a sacred space. The final destination may not necessarily be a place far from their point of departure, but an interior space: a state of being arising from the physical movement of traveling and from the traveler's inner aspirations.

In his book, *The Sacred and Profane*, philosopher Mircea Eliade defines the concept of sacred space. He claims that in traditional, religious societies, space is experienced as differentiated by the qualities of the sacred and profane, whereas for our contemporary, non-traditional and secular society, space is uniform, undifferentiated, and neutral. For Eliade, entering a sacred space allows the individual to communicate with what he or she believes to be higher levels of spiritual being, where life-enhancing qualities or regenerative forces are at work and where time may be experienced as cyclic or nonlinear. Among the essential archetypes of sacred space are the *axis mundi*, the world navel or cosmic center, and the *imago mundi*, a representation of the cosmos itself: temples, churches, and dwellings in many cultures are often conceived as small-scale models of the universe.

Eliade notes that in modern society, as individuals, we may perceive some locations as possessing special qualities due to our personal associations with them, such as the places where we were born or grew up, fell in love for the first time or experienced other major life events, or the first foreign cities we visited. He suggests that this is a degenerated form of religious experience: In these "holy" spaces of our personal universe, we may receive a revelation of a reality far different from our daily experience. [1]

The link between sacred space and the experience of non-linear time finds an intriguing parallel in travel writer Tahir Shah's concept of "hypertime," an experience of discontinuity or expansion in our perception of time, which may be triggered by the act of traveling and visiting new, unfamiliar places. Tony Hiss, author of the thought-provoking study *In Motion*, posits this expanded awareness of self in time as the core experience of what he calls "Deep Travel," an epiphany of dislocation that may be brought on even in the midst of the most mundane of journeys, such as going to our neighborhood bagel store, whenever we find ourselves momentarily torn from habit and poised in a new rapport to our environment. In such moments, old perceptual habits, like old selves, are sloughed off and the wonder of the world refreshes our senses as in childhood. From this point of view, any space that elicits such experience may become sacred in our personal associations.

Writing Exercise: The Transition

The following exercise will help you focus on the shift from "ordinary" to "meaning-enhanced" or "sacred" spaces in your own life.

For Eliade, one attribute of sacred space is that it represents a pivotal point connecting two worlds: heaven and earth; the living and the dead; the past and the present. Examples might be a sacred mountain or ziggurat connecting Earth to sky or heaven, or a portal to the underworld, like the cave of the Sybil or an underground spring, connecting the sunlit surface of the earth with lower regions. Similarly, for the Tibetans, sacred space is often denoted by the union of the elements: fire and earth in a volcano, air and earth in a grotto or cave, fire and water in a hot spring. A modern approach might hold that it is the human act of construction and memory that renders a place sacred, not the intrinsic emanations or qualities of a site. Yet studies of the emanations from the earth and atmosphere upon human health and well-being would suggest that we are subject to many subtle forms of influence that come to us from the environments in which we live. In any case, it is true that we experience the places in our lives, be they interiors or exteriors, as possessing qualities of very different natures.

For the purpose of this exercise, we will interpret sacred space as largely as possible, in terms of *personally meaningful spaces*. The pivotal point between two worlds might be something as simple as a special room in a house you were not often allowed to enter in childhood, somewhere you go in order to be alone, or a place you have always wanted to visit but never have. If you wish, however, you may also refer to a traditional sacred space you have visited.

Make a list of 10–15 "personally meaningful spaces" from your childhood or more recent experience, including travel, then choose one that might serve as the point of transition between one of the following sets of polarities:

- darkness and light
- self and others
- inside and outside
- familiar and unfamiliar
- disturbing and comforting
- crowds and solitude
- noise and silence
- water and land

- ❖ earth and sky
- ❖ heat and cold
- ❖ journey and arrival
- ❖ movement and rest
- ❖ home and away
- ❖ chaos and contemplation
- ❖ up and down
- ❖ color and bleakness
- ❖ anxiety and relief
- ❖ dream and waking
- ❖ single and married
- ❖ childhood and adolescence
- ❖ youth and maturity
- ❖ pain and relief

The list of polarities could go on forever. You'll probably think of some that are significant for you that aren't mentioned here. One of my students chose the edge of her bed as the pivotal place between the realm of sacred sleep and regeneration and her very stressful waking life as a social worker in a slum. Another woman wrote about opening a window in the house she had just inherited from her mother and rediscovering the atmosphere of her childhood, while a young man in that same class wrote about the polarity of up and down related to a nasty fall from a treehouse that marked the beginning of a turbulent adolescence.

In a class I taught for professional travel writers, one person, returning from Asia, wrote about an American-style bathtub she found in the middle of a rainforest, which for her represented the transitional space between her attachment to creature comforts back home and the rough life she had embraced as a vagabond.

Choose one polarity and picture the two states clearly in your mind, associate them each with a specific locale and a series of sense impressions, not just visual impressions. Experience the two places, the two states, the two realms as strongly different, separate, and removed from each other. First jot down quick impressions that come to you for each one, then describe each place/state of being in a short text.

Next, concentrate on the moment of transition from one realm/state of being to the other. Localize it in a specific physical setting situated between the two. What marks the point of connection or transition? What gesture, movement, or perception carries you across the threshold? What atmosphere enfolds you? What do your senses perceive? Write 100–300 words using concrete imagery to convey your experience.

The Power of Place and Places of Power

For many cultures, such as that of Tibet, some localities possess special powers, not necessarily healing powers, or rather, not *only* healing powers, that human beings may absorb and draw benefit from simply by being there, and even through contact with the ground: by treading on it, prostrating oneself upon it, eating it, touching it, preserving it in a talisman. Places of power are sites believed by some to communicate unique states of being, healing, or consciousness to those who are receptive to their influences. All religions have their places of power. According to Tibetan

Buddhist scholar Keith Dowman, who has studied sacred places of Asia in depth, the primary power of a sacred place is given by its actual placement upon the earth—with relation to longitude, latitude, magnetism, and other emanations of the earth, and only secondarily by divine consecration or human works, such as temples or other markers, upon it. Moreover, some places are believed to have memories recorded in the space itself, which may be transmitted to those who visit that place and are open to receive its energy. Writer-photographer Martin Gray, who has dedicated years of his life to exploring and documenting the sacred sites and pilgrim destinations of the entire world and its religious traditions, published his findings and photographs in an extraordinary book called: *Sacred Earth: Places of Peace and Power*. In this book, he offers the following list of sacred sites. How many of these have you visited? Are there any near your home? Have you ever taken a trip especially to see a place like one of these in the list below?[2]

- sacred mountains
- human-built sacred mountains
- sacred bodies of water
- sacred islands
- healing springs
- healing and power stones
- sacred trees and forest groves
- places of ancient mythological importance
- ancient ceremonial sites
- ancient astronomical observatories

- ❖ human-erected solitary standing stones
- ❖ megalithic chambered mounds
- ❖ labyrinth sites
- ❖ places with massive landscape carvings
- ❖ regions delineated by sacred geography (concentration of several features in one area)
- ❖ oracular caves, mountains, sites
- ❖ male deity/god shrines/yang sites
- ❖ female deity/goddess shrines/yin sites
- ❖ birthplaces of saints
- ❖ places where sages have reached enlightenment
- ❖ death places of saints
- ❖ places where relics of saints and martyrs are/were kept
- ❖ places with enigmatic fertility legends and/or images
- ❖ places with miracle-working icons
- ❖ places chosen by animals or birds
- ❖ places chosen by geomantic divinatory methods
- ❖ unique natural features
- ❖ ancient esoteric schools
- ❖ ancient monasteries
- ❖ places where dragons were slain or sighted
- ❖ places of Marian apparitions (for example, Lourdes and Fatima)

Choose one of the above and write a short travel essay, memoir, or narrative fragment. You might consider using the "Transition" exercise in framing your piece.

~

Writing the Pilgrimage, Sacred or Profane

We go on quests to fill a lack or need, to recover something lost or forgotten, whether it be tangible object or a state of mind. We make pilgrimages to keep a promise to ourselves or someone else, to reconnect to our roots: family, spiritual, or elective. We make pilgrimages to heal ourselves and make ourselves new. By writing about such experiences, we gain new insight on what we have learned from them and also transmit a spark of what we have gained to others.

Here are some suggestions for writing about such journeys, be they sacred or profane.

A Journey of Faith

Have you ever gone on a pilgrimage to a sacred shrine or site like Lourdes, Mecca, or the Wailing Wall where thousands of pilgrims congregate? Or to sacred places in nature like the Ganges or Stonehenge? Have you participated in a procession or religious celebration involving crowds such as Kumbh Mela in India, or walked St. James's Way, El Camino de Santiago in Spain? Write a narrative about your experience of the place and of the people around you. You might begin by describing why the place was important to *you* before you made your journey. What circumstances moved you to make the pilgrimage?

How did you prepare for the journey/experience? What did you bring with you? Describe your impressions and sensations using concrete imagery. Ultimately, the goal of a religious pilgrimage involves some kind of interior transformation. If you experienced such a change, try to describe it. What did you take home with you—concrete or abstract—when you left? What did you leave behind, if anything?

A Secular Pilgrimage

Have you ever made a "secular" or personal pilgrimage to a town, monument, or building connected to your family history, your own personal story, or aspirations? What pulled you there? Write a narrative to illustrate your motivation for going, your journey, and your return. Identify the elements of desire, conflict, and discovery in your experience. What new knowledge did you acquire? How were you changed?

Veer Off the Beaten Track

On your daily itinerary to work, school, or elsewhere, is there a spot just off your beaten track that you have noted as you passed that has somehow captured your imagination? It may be a street, a building, a monument, a piece of countryside, an old house, a body of water, an alley, a doorway, a gate. Make a trip to that place and then write about it, with special attention to the following details:

- ❖ When did you first notice the place? Why did it attract you?

- ❖ How did you feel when you deviated from your regular path and headed for the destination?

- ❖ What did you notice in your environment that had previously escaped your attention when only observing it from afar?

- ❖ How did it appear as you approached it from a distance?

- ❖ What signaled the moment when you actually arrived/ entered?

- ❖ What did you do there?

- ❖ How did you feel when you left and returned to your habitual path?

- ❖ Collect sensory details and images to describe the place and your response to it as accurately as you can.

❖ Is there a correspondence between this location and something in your own life, personality, or past?

For this exercise, you might also choose from the list of sacred sites given earlier. Write a narrative of your experience in 300 words using the present tense.

Journey to a Place in Time No Longer There

Think of a site or building near your home or in your life that has been radically altered from the first time you saw it. It may be an area where a house or neighborhood was torn down to make a road, shopping mall, or golf course. It may be a ruin or a ghost town, an abandoned lighthouse, something now overgrown or partly underwater. Research the area before you go by looking for old photographs, magazine illustrations, or textual descriptions or by talking to people who remember it. Then visit the place and write about your experience in 300 words. Contrast your memories of it with its actual state. You might juxtapose two or more timelines, weaving in impressions of present and past.

A Literary Pilgrimage

Virginia Woolf's first published essay, "Haworth 1904," was a description of her visit to the parsonage where the Brontës had lived. Arriving just after a snowstorm, Woolf was struck by the dreary church and churchyard, by the drabness and dinginess of the setting where the "girls" dreamed and wrote their novels that have illuminated the lives of so many readers with vivid fire. What she found most touching were a muslin dress and a pair of shoes once belonging to Charlotte, and a stool Emily took with her when rambling across the moors, so she might sit and dream while looking at the sky. If you have an opportunity, visit the house of a writer, artist, or civic leader you admire. Go through slowly—especially if you are being herded on a tour—and absorb all details you can. Don't forget to take a notebook and camera. Closely observe the details of domestic life: kitchen, bedroom, living areas, the settings, furnishings, and instruments of daily life; the books, pictures, photographs. Look out the windows to see what views they might have glimpsed, and pay very close attention to the studio, library, writing table, or room where their work was carried out. What objects, furnishings, or other aspect of the house convey to you a sense of the writer's personality? What succeeds in creating a sense of intimacy? Take note of some personal object on display and connect it to what you know or simply imagine about the writer's life or work. Use this to build your travel essay of up to 500 words, or a poem.

The Quest Narrative

The quest, one of the oldest narrative structures in the world, is simply the story of a search. The quest narrative provides the basis for many fairy tales, myths, and religious stories. Its structure is divided into three basic phases: 1. Need or Desire; 2. Conflict; 3. Breakthrough and Return. In phase one, it is a need or desire that moves the character to undertake his/her quest, setting out at a specific time from a specific place, and separating him/herself from the familiar environment.

As the action unfolds, obstacles and setbacks are encountered that attempt to deflect the quester from his/her intent, and the action rises to a central conflict or crisis in phase two. The quester's way of resolving this crisis will lead to one of four possible solutions in phase three: success, failure, stalemate, or change of direction. After experimenting with the "Transition" exercise, choose one of the pilgrimage themes also given above and write a quest narrative of 1,000–3,000 words following the pattern as explained below.

- ❖ **Phase 1: Need/Desire** The first part of your essay or narrative sets up the situation and should focus on the protagonist's motivation and intentions. If you are working in first person—who and where are you? What was the object of your quest and why was it important to you? What need or desire compelled you to make this journey? It isn't necessary to state this bluntly, you can also do it subtly with suggestion or evocation. The reader needs to understand what your goal is. Ultimately the first question that will arise in the reader's mind is, "Will the goal be achieved?" The curiosity to discover whether it will be reached or not will lead the reader on.

- ❖ **Phase 2: Conflict** What difficulties, adventures, and inner or outer struggles did you encounter on your journey? It is conflict that lends the story its momentum once the quester's desire or need has been expressed. What obstructed you or held you back on your search? What help did you receive? What forces, events, or people came to your aid or hindered you? This phase will be the most

unique part of your experience. Use storytelling techniques, imagery, attention to setting, strong active verbs,
and dialogue to create a vivid piece of writing.

❖ **Phase 3: Breakthrough** Dealing with the conflict in the
previous phase will lead to a breakthrough. By the end,
the protagonist will either have succeeded or failed to
attain the object of his quest, will have lost interest, or
perhaps the quest itself will have changed. The climax or
breakthrough should be connected to an inner transformation of the protagonist. In what way were you changed
by the experience? It is this transformation that gives
depth to the story and may be related to a larger issue,
idea, or theme in your piece that will heighten the reader's
identification with your protagonist and elevate your piece
from a personal story to something more universal.

Suggested Reading

Paulo Coelho, *The Pilgrimage*
René Daumal, *Mount Analogue*
Alexandra David-Neel, *My Journey to Lhasa*
China Galland, *Longing for Darkness*

The Writer as Flâneur

Pilgrims and questers have a well-defined approach to places and journeys. They usually know where they are going and why and have an idea of what they hope to attain by the end of their journey. There are other ways to relate to places, however, and on the opposite side of the spectrum from the pilgrim, we find the *flâneur*. In Virginia Woolf's essay, "Street Haunting," written in 1928, the author steps out to buy a pencil, leaving the cramped solitude of her writing desk on a winter evening, to become "an enormous eye," floating down the street, taking in impressions; skimming, untouched, through a series of grotesque encounters with the derelict and incongruous inhabitants of London, some of whom will later appear as characters in the crowd scenes of *Mrs. Dalloway*. Buying a pencil was, of course, only a pretext, an excuse to get out of the house and out of herself. What she really wanted to do was immerse herself in the life of the city while remaining detached from it, a theme running through many works of modernism, a literary movement which celebrated urban life in many different ways.

> I have been a camera.
> —*Katherine Mansfield*

As she drifted fancy-free through her London neighborhood, she was probably aware that she was practicing an art known to the French as *"Flânerie,"* whose devotees were called *"flâneurs"*—or aimless strollers, spectators of modern life. The feminine of this term is *"flâneuse."* There is no exact equivalent for this word in English. It is not easy to define the term or even name recognized practitioners, though both Charles Baudelaire (1821–1867) and Walter Benjamin (1892–1940) are sometimes cited as the forefathers of modern *flânerie*. English translations of *"flâneur"* tend toward the derogatory like "lounger," "loafer," even "loiterer," since our culture is suspicious of "purposeless activity." The *Merriam-Webster Dictionary* proposes "idle man about town," which may suggest either a person of leisure or simply someone without a job. And yet, the *flâneur*, argue the French, is the very opposite of idleness. He or she is, above all, an explorer of city streets, a keen spectator and reporter of urban realities. The French modernist poet, Charles Baudelaire, exalted this figure in his work as the artist-poet who dwells in the heart of the multitude and views the world from its very center while remaining incognito. Although the *flâneur*, akin to the English dandy, first arose in French literature and in the city of Paris, Walter Benjamin and later scholars have identified this figure as the soul of urban consciousness and mass culture, and even as a contemporary mode of being in the world. For Benjamin, the *flâneur* was the priest of the soul of place.[3]

The *flâneur* emerges on the scene in the mid-nineteenth century, when the urban transformations in commerce, transportation, architecture, manufacturing, and population increase began to shape cityscapes as we know them today. Old neighborhoods were torn down to create wide thoroughfares, low- and middle-income housing areas and monumental squares, where towering constructions of glass, iron, and steel glittered on the skyline. Railways streamed people and goods in and out of city centers at harrowing speeds—although some feared that such velocity might cause cerebral disorders. The air was dense with smoke and steam rather than the earthy odor of horses.

Over the next decades, horse-drawn omnibuses yielded to trams and motor vehicles, bringing new dangers in crossing the street. To say nothing of the noise, which, Benjamin tells us, was mercifully reduced by the asphalting of some roads, allowing people in cafés to converse without shouting into each other's ears. New sidewalks separated the vehicular traffic from crowds of pedestrians of all classes and professions now rubbing shoulders on the streets in unprecedented ways. For a pittance, you could travel by omnibus from one end of the city to another, from the poorest slum to the realm of the rich or vice versa, to see how the other half lived.

In the meantime, you shared a small space with other passengers at whom you gazed without ever exchanging a word, while enticing women and men winked from billboards and placards like figures in a dream, urging you to try a new tooth powder or liqueur. Jostled, nudged, prodded, and buffeted about amid an ocean of heads, individuals found themselves enclosed in their solitude, becoming, as poet Paul Valéry lamented, mere specks in a flux of anonymous particles. The milling of crowds and the meshing of social classes, the ever-changing display of manufactured goods in shop windows and market stalls gave rise to a great phantasmagoric spectacle absorbing into itself the consciousness and individuality of all its participants.

The task of the *flâneur* was to observe all this coolly, critically, from the sidelines, while leaning over a bridge, hanging out at a corner café or looking down from the open top of a double-decker bus. The *flâneur* could keep his or her identity intact or assume another. As Woolf suggests in her essay, the anonymity of the city allows us to loosen up and put on another mask if we wish. Or as Baudelaire suggested, the solitary stroller may enjoy the privilege of being oneself or someone else entirely, merging with the character of anyone at all.

The *flâneur* wanders crowded city streets, taking in images and sensations of the myriad lives around him, observing the rhythms and rituals of the city manifested by all its social classes, without ever being swept up in them. Walter Benjamin tells us that the art was born in Paris and could not have been born in Rome, where grandiose monuments and ruins impose on visitors a tourist's point of view. The true *flâneur* seeks contact with the evanescent moment and with authentic experience, preferring the old, the worn, the odd to grandeur and sparkle. Flea markets, second-hand bookstores, unlit alleys offer irresistible attractions. The city becomes a book to be read in the margins and at the same time a labyrinth to get lost in, both horizontally and vertically, while one seeks out glimpses of the old neighborhoods as they used to be, still visible beneath the new.

Street photography practiced by masters such as Eugène Atget, Berenice Abbot, Brassai, Henri Cartier-Bresson, and Vivian Maier all derive from the tradition of the *flâneur*. The Parisian *flâneur* prefers night and twilight, and while poking about gas-lit alleys, may witness criminal acts. The *flâneur* is an ardent people-watcher, a bit of a voyeur and even a spy. Stalking, searching and detection are the major themes of *flâneur* fiction, in which the hero/heroine may also be an amateur detective. Sometimes the object of the quest is an elusive love-object, as in André Breton's surrealist novel *Nadja* (1928) in which the mysterious woman pursued by the narrator is, in a way, an embodiment of the mysteries of Paris itself.

The *flâneur* has inspired various postmodern philosophers including Guy Debord, the major theorist of a movement known as "Situationism," which challenged the ideologies underlying our consumer society and the methods used by the reigning power structures to control individual behavior through the manipulation of public spaces. According to Situationists, cities and public spaces are designed to channel the masses and to generate and reinforce habits of spending and consuming.

The Situationists posed resistance by means of an act they called the *dérive*, or drift, a form of urban walking in which you let your mind go, your legs wander, and your instinctive memory lead you through the city, rediscovering recondite corners, exploring tangled networks of private narratives in motion, drifting through crowds and situations. Like the *flâneur*, the Situationist assembles his or her own inner map of the city through personal associations with places and people.

The pose of the *flâneur* offers endless inspiration for poetry, essays, and fiction. Try *flâneur* experiments on your home turf or in an unfamiliar one. Wherever practiced, they may help you see your environment as you have never seen it before.

⌒

Writing Exercises for Aspiring Flâneurs

Stroll the Streets

Go for a walk, or *dérive*, in your own neighborhood or an unfamiliar landscape. Take your notebook with you and as you wander, stop to jot down impressions as they come. Remembering Woolf's self-description as an enormous eye, consider yourself from this perspective, or if you wish, on a separate occasion, identify yourself with "an enormous ear" or "enormous nose" and see where your perceptions take you. Then go home and work your impressions into a text of 300 words or more.

Get Lost

The Flâneur Society, founded to promote the ideas of Walter Benjamin, suggests that those new to the art can make up a set of instructions for themselves on how to get lost in their own neighborhoods. For example, you might get on the next bus, get off after x-number of stops, take the first right, then when you meet a woman with a dog, stop and take stock of where you are. Sit down and write about what's happening around you. Try this yourself!

Follow a Desire Map

In *Theatre/Archaeology*, performance artists Michael Shanks and Mike Pearson describe a performance/experience based on a thematic map technique, or "desire map," in which the quester pursues traces of a particular theme, topic, or object. For their map, they chose "shoes" as the object of desire. This entailed creating an itinerary centered on shoes: finding shoes and artifacts connected to them (door mats, shoehorns, shoe sellers, second-hand shoes, shoe repair shops, discarded shoes), observing people with special footwear, observing the action of people's feet, the appearance of footprints, evidence of wear and tear caused by feet. Like the deep map, the desire map provides an interesting structural device for short fiction or essays charting the turning and twisting of the quest. Other desire map topics could be chocolate, lingerie, hats, wine, old photographs, beer mugs, auto-demolition, toy trains, dolls, or anything that appeals to you.

Street Photography

Acquaint yourself with the work of a street photographer such as Brassai or Vivian Maier, choose a few photos, and link them together with a fictional narrative. Or use photos you have taken.

Crowd Bathing

In their rambles, *flâneurs* mingle, observe, and detach themselves from crowds, although, Charles Baudelaire once warned, not everyone finds pleasure in bathing in the multitude: Enjoying crowds is an art. Finding yourself amid a swarm of other human beings can trigger our sense of the sublime, especially when an unbridled emotion sweeps through a massive gathering of people. Have you ever been in a crowd where one of these emotions dominated: joy/victory, sorrow, disappointment, disbelief, anger, terror, intense expectation, anxiety? Describe your experience.

Square Haunting

Georges Perec, the French master of constrained writing, proposes an experiment in his creative nonfiction work *An Attempt at Exhausting a Place in Paris.* For three days, he staked out a corner of the Place Saint Sulpice in Paris, moving from benches to cafés, and noting everything that transited his field of experience—buses, cars, pigeons, people, a wedding, and a funeral—documenting manifestations of real life when nothing was happening but the ordinary flux of daily reality.

Choose a place to stake out and perform a similar experiment. If the prospect of three days seems daunting, shorten the period to half a day or a few hours.

Suggested Reading

Walter Benjamin, *The Arcades Project*
André Breton, *Nadja*
Italo Calvino, *Invisible Cities*
Guy Debord, *Society of the Spectacle*
Tao Lin, *Taipei*
Georges Perec, *An Attempt at Exhausting a Place in Paris*
Edgar Allen Poe, "The Man of the Crowd"
Edmund White, *The Flâneur*
Virginia Woolf: "Street Haunting: A London Adventure"
Peter Wortsman, *Ghost Dance in Berlin*

Discovering the Soul of Place In Your Neighborhood

The exploration of your city or neighborhood as a *flâneur* makes a fine prelude for the following exercise for deep mapping your home turf and viewing it from unusual perspectives. The activity described below also draws inspiration in part from Elizabeth Vander Schaaf's "Finding the Soul of the City,"[4] a worksheet of twenty questions published online by the Louisiana Voices Folklife in Education Project. To complete a deep map, you may want to make several field trips, armed with notebook, pen, and a pair of comfortable shoes, taking notes and maybe photographs as you go. But like most exercises and activities in this book, it may also be done simply by recreating and evoking a place in memory. Once you have worked through the activity all the way to the end, you will have a very different picture—much richer, more detailed, and stratified—from your present idea of the place you choose to investigate. For a travel writing class, it makes for an interesting class project. For the writer of childhood memoirs, it will unlock a wealth of previously unrecalled details.

Identity: Place as Self

In some African cultures, the layout of villages corresponds to an idealized form of the human body. Apply this metaphor to your own town or neighborhood. Looking at a map might help you visualize it that way. Aerial photography or images from Google Earth will also provide fresh perspectives. According to your perception of the place, where is the heart? The head? How are these marked or otherwise indicated? Locate the "center"—does it correspond to either heart or head?

Identify the boundaries, which may be said to correspond to the skin separating this being from others or from the surrounding space. Examine the orifices and the routes of access. Study the circulatory system: traffic routes, railways, subways. Notice if there are any other features that might be said to correspond to human organs: brain, liver, digestive system, etc. Consider the connective tissue: what links the diverse zones?

Note the presence of water in any form: natural or artificial bodies of water, pipelines, water tanks, wells, sewage treatment plants, fountains, large concentrations of the color blue. Where are the other "watering holes" where people meet to eat and drink, bathe or swim? Note the presence of fire in any form, including steam, power plants, electric lighting, concentrations of the colors red, yellow, orange.

Examine the verticality: What areas are "up" and which ones are "down," both physically and socially? What distinguishes public space from private space in both areas? How do night and day affect the activities carried out in both areas? Who owns the streets by day and by night?

Locate the centers of money, power, religion, communication, and governance with respect to the other elements you have noted. Where are the libraries, archives, schools, universities, and the courthouse? Look for the prisons, hospitals, and cemeteries: Are they near the center or closer to the outskirts? Which places seem quiet and secluded or bustling and noisy? Do specific categories of people tend to gather in certain areas—men in groups or alone, children and teenagers, mothers with small children, students, the elderly, the homeless, vagrants? Can you find any lonely spots, no-man's lands, or dangerous areas? What sets them apart from the safe places?

Natural Cycles and Rituals

How do the cycle of seasons and the weather affect the appearance and life of the place? What's it like there when it snows or rains heavily? Where is the highest density of plant life? Do populations of woodpeckers, squirrels, or alligators share your space? Where can you see the fruits of seasons displayed? Think metaphorically: "fruits of season" may also be merchandise in shops, or different clothing or paraphernalia suited for different periods of the year, like lawn furniture, jack-o-lanterns, ski equipment. Investigate and participate in the rituals of your neighborhood. When are the festivals or religious and civic holidays celebrated? What exactly do they celebrate and why? Consider major sports, school, or political events, fairs, seasonal markets, carnivals, as well as unofficial events bringing people together. Chart the ritual itineraries used by pedestrians and motorists: children, teenagers, the routes taken by religious processions, funeral corteges, July 4th parades, marathons, protest marches, afternoon promenades, shortcuts, major traffic routes at rush hour.

Examine public art, inscriptions, monuments, and graffiti celebrating collective or personal concerns. What do they say about the place? How do the authorities make themselves heard within a given space? How do underdogs, the oppressed or demonstrators make their voices heard within the same places?

History

What names (street names, parks, etc.) are obviously historical, religious, or symbolic? Who were the original founders of the neighborhood or town? Who lived there before them? What traces have they left? Are there historical monuments or even prehistoric ones attesting to previous inhabitants, or have they been effaced? If so, when, why, and by whom? What important historical events have taken place in the area you are studying? Aside from battles, burials, or political events connected to the civic or religious life of the place, also consider the private side of local legends and gossip: scandals, tragedies, "visitations," odd occurrences, or sightings of the paranormal.

Is there a "haunted" house, a taboo or mythical place in the area? Or an unusual or weird museum? How is it considered by local inhabitants—by children especially? Do any places have special names given by locals or children? Do you note any secret or unexpected connections between sites, buildings, or neighborhoods that come as a surprise?

Once you have interrogated your environment in this way, you will have accumulated an enormous amount of information about it, an indispensable aid for making a deep map, or just getting a sense of the soul of place operating in every location and activity. If you are a fiction writer working with a large canvas, this approach to research will give you some ideas about how to construct vivid settings and bring them alive with concrete details. Or it simply might help you rediscover places you have never considered as a source of material for your writing.

Years ago in my hometown, on the main street across from the movie theater, there was an old-timey newsstand selling magazines, paperbacks, pinwheels, and in the back, out of reach, men's magazines in brown paper wrappers. It was the only place open on Sundays, besides church, within a radius of fifty miles. By some miracle, you could buy *The New York Times* there, a welcome sign for some of us that real life still existed farther north. A smell of tobacco, buttered popcorn, fresh newsprint, and cotton candy hung heavy in the air. Near the door stood a bronze spittoon. I used to go there with a friend after school on Mondays to pick up the Sunday *Times* and lug it home, where my culture-starved mother and I devoured the pages devoted to books, theater, music, and cuisine. That newsstand is a part of my personal mythography, even though I have never written about the place. It figures in some very fine poems by poet laureate Charles Wright, a native of my town, who has described it as the unlikely site of teenage epiphanies. Wright's whole work, in fact, could be read as a deep map of the towns, landscapes, and moods of Appalachia. By investigating your neighborhood, you may find a few forgotten corners that may turn out to be treasure troves.

Writing Exercise: Deep Mapping Your Neighborhood

In an extraordinary short story/prose poem entitled "In the Heart of the Heart of the Country" published in 1968, William Gass portrays life in the unnamed town of "B.... Indiana" as experienced through the persona of a "poet-narrator" in "retirement from love." The plotless narrative is constructed from blocks of short passages each with its own title, mingling descriptive, narrative, and expository styles, character sketches, and interior monologues, each with its own subtitle: "Wires," "Weather," "Business People," "The Church," etc. The story has been called a catalogue of descriptions, even a list of lists, a ramble through the psyche of its narrator, and a lethal portrayal of solitude in the rural Midwest. The structure of this story/prose poem fits well with the deep map exercise, and offers insights on organizing material gathered.

After investigating your town or neighborhood, employing the ideas given above, identify a few categories of interest from the material you gathered for your deep map. Use these as your subheadings/titles and piece together your essay/narrative as a patchwork.

Linda Lappin

Where to Look for the Genius Loci

The *genius loci*, is, as you may have guessed, everywhere. The following are just a few suggestions of where to go looking for it. They reflect my own subjective and limited experience shaped by a few specific environments: the Southeastern USA, Italy, France, and other places I have lived and traveled. The places *you* have lived and traveled may be quite different, so follow your instincts when hunting for the soul of place.

Markets

I love visiting outdoor markets when I travel, and also discovering new ones at home. Markets, claims Lewis Mumford in *The City*, sprang up at crossroads very early in urban history and were probably the forerunners of cities themselves, so they have a strong connection with the soul of place. They aren't only an excellent source for fresh food or cheap goods, but also intensely packed story-places. For me, observing people at work is part of the enjoyment of market day. I like to study the dexterity of the fishmonger as he slices up soles into filets with a long, clean swipe of a knife, or the woman at the vegetable stand trimming artichokes with such speed, it looks like a sleight-of-hand trick, or the heavyset men shouldering sides of beef from a van, their white jackets smeared with blood. Then there are the old ladies, picking out coins from their worn change purses, or the housewives listening intently while the butcher gives them a tip or two, tilting their heads to one side, knowing that their recipe is better than his, but still willing to

83

learn something new. Markets also track the seasons. You know it's spring in Rome when frothy yellow mimosa branches, bundles of wild asparagus, and *agretti* make their first appearance on the stalls and stands.

The literature of travel abounds with descriptions of outdoor markets. Novelists with an eye for locale, from James Joyce to Anita Brookner and Shirley Hazzard, have celebrated the exotic appeal of fairs and market areas. A profusion of flowers, fruit, fish, herbs, antiques, old clothes or trinkets displayed on stalls or simply spread on tarps on the ground are all typical market wares that delight our senses. They speak of plenty, of the enchantment of "homemade" or "homegrown"; they connect us to the most basic processes of our physical life and signal changing seasons. Transactions with vendors remind us that we are dependent on others who produce or grow what we need. Not only sounds, smells, and colors, but also the close physical contact of crowds contribute to the feeling of festivity on market day. Some markets can be overwhelming, like the wholesale meat market in Athens, then without refrigeration, into which I stumbled one day in August with the temperature above 100 degrees.

The following passage by D.H. Lawrence taken from *Sea and Sardinia* gives an example of vivid descriptive technique in recreating the atmosphere of a farmers' market. Note that the text is structured as a list. Note also the use of color. It reads like a painting.

> Peasant women, sometimes barefoot, sat in their tight little bodices and voluminous, coloured skirts behind the piles of vegetables, and never have I seen a lovelier show. The intense deep green of spinach seemed to

predominate, and out of that came the monuments of curd-white and black-purple cauliflowers: but marvellous cauliflowers, like a flower-show, the purple ones intense as great bunches of violets. From this green, white, and purple massing struck out the vivid rose-scarlet and blue crimson of radishes, large radishes like little turnips, in piles. Then the long, slim, gray-purple buds of artichokes, and dangling clusters of dates, and piles of sugar-dusty white figs and sombre-looking black figs, and bright burnt figs: basketfuls and basketfuls of figs. A few baskets of almonds, and many huge walnuts. Basket-pans of native raisins. Scarlet peppers like trumpets: magnificent fennels, so white and big and succulent: baskets of new potatoes: scaly kohlrabi: wild asparagus in bunches, yellow-budding *sparacelli*: big, clean-fleshed carrots: feathery salads with white hearts: long, brown-purple onions and then, of course pyramids of big oranges, pyramids of pale apples, and baskets of brilliant shiny *mandarini*, the little tangerine oranges with their green-black leaves. The green and vivid-coloured world of fruit-gleams I have never seen in such splendour as under the market roof at Cagliari: so raw and gorgeous.[5]

—D.H. Lawrence, *Sea and Sardinia*

Writing Exercise: Describe a Market

What better way to discover the soul of a city than to visit its market to see local foods, clothing, household wares, and handicrafts? Hundreds of guidebooks have been published dedicated to street markets around the world, such as Dixon and Ruthanne Long's *Markets of Paris;* Sandy Price's *The Flea Markets of France;* and Karen Seigner's *Markets of New York City;* along with dozens of small pamphlets and publications dedicated to local farmers' markets all over the USA. Visit a market or popular shopping area in your town or in a foreign city. If possible visit more than once at different hours of the day, investigating these aspects:

❖ Where is it located with respect to the rest of the town?

❖ How do most people reach the market?

❖ How is it arranged? What areas are set aside only for vendors?

❖ What side activities are taking place, such as private transactions at the edges?

❖ What stalls most attract you? Are the goods local or imported?

❖ How do the displays reflect the particular season or moment of the year?

❖ What things strike you as most exotic or representative of that particular place or time?

❖ How are goods displayed: roughly or to enhance attractiveness and entice buyers?

❖ Take note of vendors and customers—clothes, manner of transaction, and interaction. In many markets "street criers" and "hawkers" still use special patter to attract buyers.

❖ What happens around closing time? What is left in the aftermath?

List details for each of the five senses conveying your impressions, then write a descriptive passage of 300 words. Try to note as many sounds and smells as you can. Create your description by using the list technique illustrated in the example above or focus on a single item that you noticed or purchased and build an entire passage around it.

Or, make a special trip to a market selling food products, the more exotic the better. Choose some food items you haven't tried before. Ask the seller for tips on how to prepare them, if necessary. Take them home, make yourself a meal, and then write 300 words about the experience.

Public Parks and Gardens

The relationship between place and story was a subject of keen exploration in baroque architecture and garden design. Many of the great Italian gardens of the sixteenth century, like Villa Lante or Bomarzo, were constructed with specific stories in mind, such as the Descent to the Underworld, the Garden of Eden, the Myth of Narcissus, the Birth of the Muses. Garden designers then, as now, worked with many elements in shaping a narrative: the landscape and the layout of pathways; the choice of plants for their color, shade, seasonal appearance, leaf textures, shadows, and attractiveness to birds and butterflies. Architectural structures and artistic embellishments were also important: stairways, walls, gazebos, fountains, statuary, or inscriptions. Italian gardens of the baroque period were sometimes intended to celebrate the personality or exploits of their owners, and occasionally included special measures, like astrological references in the positioning of plants or statuary, to promote health, compensate a weakness of character, or even alter fate. Such gardens were not illustrations of stories but true landscape narratives in which the visitor, while wandering a labyrinthine passageway, drinking from a fountain, or resting in the shade of an exotic tree, became the protagonist of a three-dimensional, ever-changing and unique picture book, meant to lead him or her to a deeper understanding of the self. Such ideas came to influence garden design in later centuries, including the designs of New York's Central Park and Disneyland.

Gardens invite us to awaken our senses to nature and intensify our physical experience of the world: they are far more than collections of plants. The formal gardens of Versailles; the rose gardens adored by the English; Italian gardens with fake grottoes, simulated ruins, wooded areas and labyrinths; Japanese tea gardens or Zen plots of raked gravel; all are attempts at illustrating the fine balance between nature and the human mind. Gardens may conceal secret doctrines, enhance political power, or even suggest a route to enlightenment. To visit such gardens is to interact with their magic on many levels, to undergo a transformation by means of an enchantment in which all the senses participate.

Writing Exercise: Explore a Garden

Explore a garden or public park area—it may be just a bench on a corner under a shady tree, a secluded spot at the end of a street. Pay attention to the following details:

- ❖ What looks wild? What looks cultivated?
- ❖ How do water, sun, shade, rock, soil, and vegetation work together to create an impression?
- ❖ How do color, texture, smell, and movement of plants contribute to the overall impression?
- ❖ Do pathways, trails, vistas, or the layout of the garden seem to draw you toward certain places in the garden, to panoramas, secret places, bodies of water, or architectural features (pavilion, fountain, tea house, bridge), art works (sundial), or displays of plants?
- ❖ Are you aware of any symbolism at work in the garden at any level?
- ❖ Are there animals or birds?
- ❖ If there are other people in the park or garden during your visit, what are they doing?

❖ Is there a place where you locate its spirit—is it retiring, or extroverted, joyous or subtle?

❖ If there are statues, what do they *see?* What perspectives are they pointing out to you?

Take your time to explore. Then write a travel essay of your visit. Bring in all the senses.

In a short text of up to 100 words, describe the smell or taste of something growing in a garden.

Or write a story with a scene that takes place in a garden.

Or imagine the garden *itself* as a story.

Suggested Reading

Jorge Luis Borges, "Elegy for a Park"
Duncan Brine, *The Literary Garden*
Jean-Cristophe Napias, *Quiet Corners of Paris*
Vivian Russell, *Edith Wharton's Italian Gardens*
David A. Slawson, *Secret Teachings in the Art of Japanese Gardens*
Edith Wharton, *Italian Villas and their Gardens*

Statues

On the outskirts of my hometown in East Tennessee was an old-fashioned market called Honest John's, selling baskets of peaches in summer, pumpkins and ten-gallon jugs of apple cider in fall. Out front stood a giant Indian brave, at least twenty feet tall, made of terracotta. Returning from vacations, weary of the endless car ride in the back of our station wagon, my brother and I would be on the alert miles ahead. Sighting the Indian down the road was the sign that we were home, and he seemed to greet us solemnly and welcome us back. Later, in the sixties, when the malls were built in that area, this piece of genuine American folk art vanished for a time, to the dismay of many children. He had lent a dash of color and fantasy to that flat, anonymous landscape. After a long absence, he recently returned, shabbier and more fragile-looking, but still standing tall, overlooking the parking lot of a used car dealer.

Such statues are repositories of the spirit of place. The Statue of Liberty, the Moais of Easter Island, the angel of Berlin, the vanished Colossus of Rhodes, and Bernini's winged figures on Rome's Bridge of Angels, all welcome newcomers and homecomers, protect the community, and warn those with evil intentions to be on their guard. Guardian statues are also a fixture outside temples, cemeteries, cathedrals, and shrines. Often legend holds that they are endowed with powers. Many are still the destinations of pilgrimages, like the reclining Buddha of Bangkok or the Egyptian sphinx.

Statues are often intended to fit into a specific environment where pre-existing elements such as landscape features, architecture, sunlight, wind, or the presence of other artworks contribute to their meaning. Once removed from their context, they may lose some of their original power and significance but gain new ones.

Writing Exercise

Is there a guardian statue somewhere in your town? Or perhaps you have seen one in a museum, no longer associated with its original context. Investigate its history. What does it commemorate? What power does it represent? What view unfolds before its eyes? What scenes might it have witnessed in previous eras?

Write a descriptive text of 250 words or write a short narrative from the statue's point of view.

Fiction writers: write a scene in which a character discovers or talks to a statue.

Patron Saints and Other Protectors

When I moved to a medieval village in central Italy, I soon noticed that its patron saint, Archangel Michael, was a ubiquitous presence. His icon hangs over a narrow cobbled street overlooking a treacherous precipice, where—according to the annals of local gossip—a villager once committed suicide. His name is embedded in street names like "Ser Michelino." Crude life-sized statues made of plastic or wood are tucked into dark corners of the village's churches. He appears in frescoes on crumbling walls. Nearly every home has a small icon, postcard, or embroidery depicting him, hanging over the door or propped up on the mantelpiece.

Once a year on the eighth of May, a statue of Michael is removed from a church and carried through the streets down into a canyon and up to a chapel carved in a cliff on the other side. A thick tangle of legends, customs, and beliefs are attached to this effigy, blending myth, faith, superstition, and even civic power, for as late as the early 1960s, one long-time resident told me, public announcements by the town crier were made in the names of the President of the Italian Republic, the Mayor, and Archangel Michael. In a nearby village, a statue of Michael stood over the stocks situated in the main square, where people were put to public shame in relatively modern times for acts of adultery or petty theft.

Iconography connected to Michael shows a warrior angel, clad in armor, holding a lance or sword with which he pins a writhing demon to the ground. In his left hand, he holds a scale, with which he weighs rights and wrongs. Now he is recognized as the patron saint of law enforcement officers, though this is a recent dedication, dating from the 1950s, for he triumphs over the snake of evil. The legends surrounding his origins, both Christian and pagan, are connected to grottos and caves, to subterranean spaces, to the womb of the earth, for Michael's first recorded appearance was in a cave.

Mythologists trace Michael back to the figure of Hermes, traditionally represented by a snake wrapped around his staff, symbolizing the powers of healing, and to the Egyptian god Thoth, the weigher of souls. The cult of Michael is prominent in France where one of Michael's most alluring statues may be seen above the fountain of Place St. Michel in Paris. The cult may have been brought by Lombard soldiers as they traveled southwards to Italy on their way to the crusades. Throughout the remote mountain villages of central Italy you will find chapels and monasteries dedicated to him, sometimes carved in the clefts of cliffs or wedged in between boulders. Very often you will find traces of him in places where geo-thermal phenomena are present, associated in medieval times with demonic powers that the archangel's presence helps keep in check.

Writing Exercise: Interrogate an Icon

Identify a "protector"—statue or icon—in your own town, or elsewhere. Make a visit to it with the sole purposes of observing it and receiving its influence. Study its position in relation to the houses, the town center, adjacent sites of power or worship, and its placement within the general landscape or interior setting. If possible, try to research any stories, legends, or superstitions connected to it, or historical events that occurred in the surroundings. Ask yourself: What feelings and values were attached to it when it was first created and placed in its setting? What conditions are attached to it now? What activities unfold around it today?

Don't be afraid to open your mind to spontaneous promptings or even an inner conversation with the figure itself. Don't censor impressions that may come in this way as you tune into your unconscious.

Use this material for a fragment of memoir or literary travel essay.

You might also connect this exercise with a quest or pilgrimage, or combine it with a postcard narrative.

From Poetic Creation to Political Reality

Protective guardians need not be of religious origin, like Archangel Michael. They need not be the result of a collective process operating through centuries in the form of myth-making; they may also be the product of a single mind, of an artist or writer. An interesting example of how the imaginary creations of poets and writers may tap into the soul of place and have an impact on political reality and historical events is illustrated by the story of Henry Wadsworth Longfellow's fictional heroine, Evangeline, who represents the spirit of the Acadian Canadians and their territory.

One of the most deplorable episodes in the history of the British colonization of North America was the deportation of the French-speaking Acadians from the fertile territory of Grand-Pré in Nova Scotia during the period 1755–1763, which provides the background for Longfellow's celebrated narrative poem *Evangeline*, written in 1847. In the poem, the Acadian Evangeline is cruelly separated from her lover Gabriel during the deportation. She spends her life searching for him, becomes a sister of mercy, and at last, while treating victims of a smallpox epidemic in Philadelphia, finds him among her dying patients.

In the century following the publication of Longfellow's poem, the figure of Evangeline became a cult image focusing the energies of the dispersed community, and contributed significantly to recreating its sense of collective identity. The emotions and identity generated by Evangeline spurred many Acadians to return to the territories from which their forefathers and foremothers had been ousted and to reassert their claims and ties to the land. Visitors today to the Grand-Pré National Historic Site—or to other monuments and museums attesting to the Acadian heritage—will discover books, pamphlets, films, statues, newspapers, songs, costumes, historical re-enactments, souvenirs, clothing, recipes, and even food products, all commemorating Evangeline and the values she represents of loyalty, purity, and steadfastness. Many tourists would probably be amazed to discover that this mother of Acadian identity is a purely fictitious being and yet she is mainly responsible for the very real rebirth of Acadian national sentiment in modern times.

In her study, *Postcards from Acadie*, Canadian ethnographer and historian Barbara Le Blanc traces this fascinating process from the historical reality of the deportation to the genesis of Longfellow's poem, and its unforeseeable, long-term impact on

Canadian history, geography, and economics. She shows how Longfellow, by giving voice to the spirit of this land and people through the figure of Evangeline, created a place of pilgrimage in the New World that was destined to become a shrine of sacred memory, a thriving tourist attraction to exploit, and a healing fount of empowerment.

Writing Exercise: Local Characters

Investigate a local monument in your town, or elsewhere commemorating a real or fictitious person or "character." How have the life, legend, or achievements of that individual affected the community? What traces are left in the names of streets, shops, or locales? Recipes? Customs? Reenactments or pageants? Souvenirs for sale? Try to trace the story to its origins, distinguishing fact from fiction and write a short travel essay of 1,000 words. Or write a fictional account of an episode connected to the person's life.

Stations and Locomotion

Nothing defines a town so much as its central train or bus station: welcoming you upon arrival and bidding you goodbye. Visit a train, bus, or metro station for the sake of describing it, without having to make a journey. You will see how differently the place will appear to you if you aren't running to hop on a train or bus. Leisurely explore the areas designated for information and ticket booths, waiting areas, restrooms, shopping, eating, platforms or boarding areas, and the area outside the station. Stations have their micro communities of workers, commuters, misfits, panhandlers, and other regulars who are part of the soul of place, so include them in your observations.

Observe what people are doing. Notice the way they're dressed and what they're carrying: those in the throes of furious rush, others lingering over a coffee at a sit-down café. See what's getting loaded onto baggage cars. The strangest thing I ever saw being loaded onto a train was at Rome's Termini Station, where dozens of boxes containing large live snakes and another series of boxes containing live white mice were waiting to be put on the train. The station attendants stood around, eyeing this cargo circumspectly. You could see the snakes trying to uncoil within their cramped space. The mice scrabbled about in their boxes, scenting, no doubt, their enemies nearby. "Suppose the train derails?" I asked myself. Fortunately, it didn't.

Focus on one or two people you have noticed who seem representative of the following categories:

❖ commuter

❖ leisure traveler

❖ railway/subway official/guard

❖ panhandler

❖ people with pets, unusual luggage, or unusual clothes

❖ people who have missed their connection

❖ solitary traveler

❖ station habitué

❖ suspicious individual

Build a story around two of these figures on the themes of "escape," "reunion," "goodbye," "late," "theft," and "identity."

Your Fellow Passengers

Traveling on subway cars seems to promote a sense of utter anonymity among passengers, whereas sharing the same space in a bus or railway car at times can create a sense of community, complicity, or even solidarity—especially when problems occur. For years, every morning, I have taken a bus to work, from the main square of a rural village to the nearest town. At that hour of the morning, still too early for office workers or shop clerks to be traveling to their jobs, the passengers are students and teachers going to school, cleaning ladies or handymen en route to work, or—very often—older people on their way to the hospital for a check-up, or to visit relatives there. With the exception of students, most of these passengers are older women who regularly use that service, always at the same time of day. For those regular travelers, the bus is like a club meeting where they exchange gossip, news, opinions, and recipes, and generally catch up with what's happening in the town and in the world, and have their say. Conversations inevitably rotate around: health—who's in the hospital having what done to them, the local priest, politics, and lastly, what it was like in the old days. If you have the opportunity, take a ride on a commuter bus, coach, or train frequently used by regulars and study their interaction. Keep your ears and eyes open. Write down some dialogue you overhear.

Writing Exercise: A Night Journey

Elizabeth Bishop's narrative poem "The Moose" vividly recreates a long night journey by bus from a sleepy province of fish, tea, and bread, southward, along the northeastern coast toward Boston. She describes the dented, battered vehicle trundling through the changing landscape and the somnolent atmosphere on the bus itself: the gossiping, dreaming, snoring passengers whose journey is interrupted in the middle of the night by the appearance of a moose in the road. It took Bishop over twenty years to finish the poem; some critics believe the unnamed coastal area is Nova Scotia, where Bishop was sent to live with her grandmother after her mother was institutionalized. The journey in the poem suggests her restless search for "home."

Night journeys often evoke a sense of excitement: the expectation that we will greet the dawn from a very different location than our usual one; the enjoyment of traveling under the cover of darkness while others sleep; the eerie nocturnal transformations made by moonlight in the landscape or cityscape; the uncertainty and even the dangers of night travel. Turkish novelist Orhan Pamuk in his novel *The New Life* describes pages and pages of endless nocturnal bus rides interrupted by apocalyptic wrecks.

Use the memory of a journey by night with any form of transportation as the subject of an essay, poem, or story. Or, if you can't remember one, take a night trip now and write about it.

Suggested Reading

Elizabeth Bishop, "The Moose"
Paul Bowles, *The Sheltering Sky*

Antoine De Saint-Exupery, *Night Flight*
Orhan Pamuk, *The New Life*

Writing Exercise: Getting About

Bicycles in Amsterdam or Shanghai, rickshaws and *tuk-tuks* in Southeast Asia, gondolas in Venice, donkeys in Santorini, *motorini* in Rome, camels in the Sahara, houseboats and barges on the Seine, the elevated trains of Tokyo—these are subjects for postcards, but have you actually ever viewed your own city from one? Explore a place you know well using alternative transportation, such as:

❖ bicycle

❖ boat

❖ rickshaw

❖ balloon

❖ glider/hang glider

❖ animal or animal conveyance

❖ scooter

❖ rollerblades/ice skates

❖ buggy, cart, carriage

❖ bus

❖ other

Note the following:

❖ What new perspective is allowed by your means of transport?

❖ Are you closer or more distant to buildings/streets/crowds?

❖ What atmospheres strike you most vividly as you roll, glide, or jostle by?

Describe your speed, the physical sensations of movement, and any related sense impressions: smells, sounds, sights. Try to use concrete imagery as described earlier in this book. Take fifteen minutes to write a narrative about your trip, including all the sense details you can, and the precise moments of departure and arrival—without necessarily putting events in chronological order.

Or write a story that takes place entirely on a vehicle in movement.

The above exercise combines well with the exercises in Chapter One and with the suggestions given in "Discovering the Soul of Place of Your Neighborhood" at the beginning of this chapter. Or consider using a postcard narrative.

Writing Exercise: Drivers

Very often our first encounter with a local upon arriving in a new place is with the bus or taxi driver who transports us into the mesh of life at our destination: New York cab drivers, London cabbies, Roman bus drivers, and Venetian gondoliers have inspired memorable scenes in fiction and film, some sinister, others comic or romantic. Recall an arrival in a new place when you met up with a memorable driver. Write a narrative of 500 words. Include any of the following:

❖ appearance, smell, sound, etc. of the vehicle

❖ your physical sensation of the ride

❖ driver's clothes, idiosyncrasies, attitude, and expertise

❖ your itinerary and the trip itself

❖ your interaction with driver or other passengers

❖ events along the way

❖ your arrival at your destination

❖ paying the fare

Dramatize moments in your narrative with dialogue. Aim for a funny, ominous, or ironic conclusion.

Suggested Reading

Elizabeth Bowen, "The Demon Lover"
J. D. Salinger, *The Catcher in the Rye*

Writing Exercise: Departing

The train pulls out from the station, the ferry raises anchor as the engines churn, the bus trundles around the curve, the flight attendant shuts the hatch as you prepare for take-off. At that precise moment, however painfully or joyfully, your attention is torn from where you have been as it anticipates where you will be next. Recreate a moment of departure with yourself as the traveler. What are you carrying away with you physically and mentally? Feel the handle of your suitcase in your hand. Feel the thrust and flow of the vehicle as you are being transported on the ground, on water, or in the air. Your body registers movement in many ways. Now, focus on the person or place that is *losing you* and describe the parting from their point of view. Write a farewell letter to the place, or one to yourself from the place.

Suggested Reading

Donald Justice, "On the Night of the Departure by Bus"

Telling Time

Prominent in most urban areas, there'll probably be a "time-keeper" of some kind, from decorative sundials to flashing digital screens. Every day thousands of tourists in Venice crane their necks to admire the clock tower of Piazza San Marco where, upon the stroke of the quarter hour, two bronze figures swing out from theirs doors to bang a bell with their hammers. Yet their mechanical dance is not as captivating as the solemn tolling of the Campanile across from the tower, calling the faithful to vespers. I have seen crowds in the piazza mesmerized, momentarily paralyzed, by the booming of those bells that have the power to arrest all movement in the piazza. At the first deafening clang, everyone stops, looks up, thrilled by the overwhelming reverberation filling the air. In astonished silence, all are united by a moment of shared awareness. Seconds later, the magic fades and the bustling resumes.

Is there a "time-keeper" in your life other than your own alarm clock? Maybe it's a factory whistle, the roar of traffic at peak hours, birdsong, church bells, the bugle at a nearby barracks, or the call of the muezzin at dawn. It could be a plant in your garden, like a night-blooming Cereus, counting the evening hours before it withers and drops from its stalk, or a constellation rising over the crest of a hill. It could also be an animal or a person: your pet scratching at the bedroom door wanting in or out, or, as in my Rome apartment, the upstairs neighbor knocking her broom on the railing of her balcony at five o'clock in the morning.

Make a point of noticing how different "clocks" in your environment keep track of time or signal cyclic events taking place around you. You'll probably find a whole mesh of sounds and movements marking the passing of time.

Writing Exercise: Clock the Hours

Write a lyric essay or poem that follow the events of a single day/night in your life, counterpointed by awareness of different "time-keepers" as discussed above.

Write a short story of up to 3,000 words taking place over the course of a single unit of time. You might find inspiration in two great classics in which awareness of church bells or clock towers forms the background for the characters' actions and thoughts: James Joyce's *Ulysses* and Virginia Woolf's *Mrs. Dalloway*.

Write 300 words on the topic of "bad timing."

Make a deep map of "time-keepers" in your immediate environment.

Writing Exercise: Weather and Seasonal Changes

Describe the view from your window or the roof of your house in different weather conditions or seasons.

Ruins

The city of Rome has been compared to a palimpsest—a continual rewriting of one text upon another with superimposed layers of buildings upon buildings, crumbling away at times to reveal fragments of the ancient core moldering beneath. Over centuries, each successive generation of inhabitants has found a way to adjust their lives to the looming presence of what remains of the past. The ruins of Rome were documented in the eighteenth century by the Venetian-born artist, Giambattista Piranesi (1720–1778), in two famous series of engravings, "Views of Rome" and "Prisons." Piranesi claimed that his main purpose was to record a visual testimony of the monumental past threatened by the wear of time, and even worse, by the greed of property owners intent on secretly dismantling old buildings to sell the rubble for modern constructions. Piranesi made his living by selling these prints to tourists, and his work was soon in great demand. In order to satisfy his clients' tastes, he tended to romanticize and enhance his depictions so that some of his most famous prints are completely imaginary views. Typically, his engravings of Rome are cluttered with a jumble of vases,

> Ruins give us pleasure by launching us into infinity.
>
> *—Bernardin de Saint-Pierre*

obelisks, inscriptions, busts, and often contain sweeping vistas, distorted perspectives, jagged lines, swirling volumes, all dwarfing the ghostly presence of tiny, alienated human figures. His work is now seen as a transition from the Enlightenment to Pre-Romanticism and was so renowned and influential that Byron, Keats, and Goethe came to Italy to see the monuments for themselves. Goethe, as it turns out, was disappointed that the real monuments were not nearly as fantastical as they had been portrayed in Piranesi's pictures.

Whether we are attracted to abandoned abbeys, Mayan pyramids, bombed out neighborhoods in Rome or Beirut, deserted farmhouses on the prairie, the industrial ruins of Detroit, or nuclear disaster sites like Chernobyl, our appreciation of ruins is a legacy of both the Renaissance and of the Romantic Age. Ruins help us situate ourselves in a vanishing landscape and contemplate our own mortality while enjoying a sense of the sublime. They are places of mystery that allow us to escape from the monotony of modern metropolises.

Writing Exercise: Listen to a Ruin

In his famous essay, "Landscape and Character," novelist Lawrence Durrell claims that people are an expression of their habitat, and that the role of the travel writer is to identify the special quality in the landscape that is imprinted on local residents and their culture. To find this quality, he suggests sitting attentively in places, a process he defines as "quiet identification." If this sounds intriguing, try the following exercise.

Visit a ruin. Interpret the word "ruin" liberally. It may be an abandoned house, a ghost town, an industrial ruin, a house in Pompeii, a pyramid, or your backyard childhood swing set.

First, let yourself take in the scene without trying to force images of what you *think* life might have been like in the past. Do not block them, however, if images start rushing to the fore of your consciousness. Let your curiosity and instinct lead you to places that will resonate for you. Try to imagine what has caused the place to look as it does today. As you ramble about, you will probably find yourself attracted by a detail or two that you should now focus on. What function did that detail serve in the remote past? Let images come to mind and feelings emerge as you dwell on one or two details. If you can, sit for a while and listen to the place and atmosphere, then when you return to your writing desk, remember yourself as you circulated in the ruins, and jot down your impressions. Use this to write a lyric or personal travel essay of 1,000–1,500 words,

Or write an ode, or a lyric essay following the ode's pattern.

Or write a short story taking place there in the past, weaving in two timelines, past and future.

Research the place to gather historical information, then write an essay combining facts and personal impressions.

Fountains

Forever, it seems, tourists have tossed coins over their left shoulders into the Trevi fountain in Rome to guarantee their return to the Eternal City. A current belief holds that tossing two coins leads to new romance while three will bring marriage or divorce, depending on your marital status at the time. The custom of paying tribute to water with money is a practice traced back to both ancient Romans and Celts, and possibly the Etruscans, who honored the ground with a similar practice. They threw coins into holes along the road in gratitude to the gods for being allowed to walk there. Throwing money into fountains has become so widespread throughout the contemporary world that it is difficult to find a public fountain nowadays anywhere *without* coins on the bottom. These traditions celebrate the soul of place, and emphasize the connection between fertility and water, the central belief of ancient pagan cults throughout the world known as "the cult of the waters." Sacred bodies of water, fountains, springs, and wells continue to draw pilgrims from many traditions the world over in search of healing, well-being, fertility, and spiritual regeneration. We go to the beach for the same reasons.

What can be more vital to a community than its source of water, symbolized by decorative fountains flowing abundantly? What can be more deadly than when the water is tainted with disease? The questions of "Where does your water come from? Where does it go?" can lead to eye-opening surprises.

Rome is famous for its fountains great and small, from the magnificent works by renowned artists like Bernini to small gorgon masks or bizarre recumbent figures, bearded with ferns, whistling water through pursed lips in the silence of obscure courtyards. Fountains may symbolize life, power, generation, generosity, abundance, love, and enlightenment. They make a perfect subject for meditation or a setting for an epiphany.

Writing Exercise: Fountains

Find a fountain in your town that you consider somehow "refreshing." Think freely: maybe it's a drinking fountain in a school hall, a tap connected to a public water source, a fire hydrant, a decorative fountain, a garden hose, a well with a bucket, or an old fashioned "soda fountain." Write a lyric essay about something that happened to you there involving the concepts "refreshment," "coolness," "thirst," "need," and "desire."

Write a scene from a story in which a character relieves his thirst by drinking from a fountain.

Write a short piece of 300 words in which a fountain has a symbolic meaning.

Trash

Archaeologists and anthropologists agree: trash is a worthy subject, perhaps the most fascinating of our era. Truly, one man's trash is another man's treasure. Non-degradable garbage from events like political conventions, concerts, and football games is packaged nowadays and sold as "art" or souvenirs. The strangest thing I have ever seen cast out into the trash piled near a dumpster was a larger than life-size papier-mâché lion and two Corinthian columns, which had been left behind when a small circus pulled out of town. Keep your eyes open while walking down the street. Castoffs may have a story to tell. Dada poet Elsa Von Freytag Loringhoven used castoff objects to make her famous sculptures and body art. She was especially fond of pieces of metal, like bottle caps or twists of wire that had been flattened by cars running over them, for in this condition they expressed, in her view, the essence of modern metropolitan life. From Marcel Duchamp to Jeff Koons, artists have rummaged through garbage for "found art" and inspiration. Writers may also dig up something worthwhile too.

Writing Exercise: Your Garbage

Documentary filmmaker Gaby Geuter sifted through Carlos Castaneda's garbage to penetrate the secrets of the mysterious writer-guru in the months preceding his death. It was partly from the crumpled medical prescriptions and insulin syringes she found there that she constructed her *Filming Castaneda.*

Without having to go poking through someone's else's garbage, you might investigate your own. What does your trash say about you? Reconstruct a day in your life from the evidence in your wastepaper basket or kitchen garbage can.

One writing teacher I know has his students go searching through garbage on the street to collect objects for collages that they will later turn into short stories. If the idea appeals, try it, but remember to wear sturdy protective gloves. Or go rummaging in boxes and trunks in your basement or attic and write 1,000 words about what you find.

More Writing Exercises:

Write about something valuable or mysterious you found in the trash. Or write about something valuable you accidentally threw away.

Nothing is more forlorn than a tennis shoe or motorcycle glove lying by the roadside, obviously tossed from a passing vehicle. I often wonder: how did that end up there? And where is its mate? Write a short story about a castoff article of clothing you find on the street.

⌒

Bringing It All Together: Final Projects

Focus on one (or more of the following) encountered while exploring a neighborhood in your city:

* animal
* plant
* building
* street or square
* body of water
* bridge
* statue
* park or garden
* agricultural area
* port, shipyard, pier
* train or bus station
* prison
* temple /church/place of worship
* tomb or cemetery
* private home
* door or gate
* parking area
* abandoned area, ruin

- ❖ Laundromat
- ❖ bar and grill, truck stop, all night café, pub, fast food
- ❖ industrial area
- ❖ pool hall
- ❖ hairdresser/barbershop
- ❖ public pool, gym
- ❖ public restroom
- ❖ rest stop
- ❖ zoo, stable, pet store
- ❖ skating rink
- ❖ cinema, theater
- ❖ police station, military base
- ❖ market, grocery, bakery, butcher, pharmacy
- ❖ feed store, hardware store
- ❖ subway, metro stop
- ❖ library, archive, art gallery, museum, bookshop, music store, newsstand
- ❖ shopping mall
- ❖ hospital, psychiatric ward
- ❖ haunted house/evil place
- ❖ funeral home, morgue

Choose one of the above as expressive of the soul of place of your town or neighborhood, and write a passage of 300 words. Or:

1. Using the point of view of one or more places listed above, write a first-person text of 50–100 words per place in the present tense.

2. Write a text of 50–100 words in the second person.

3. Use the third person and present tense to write a narrative passage set in one of the places listed.

4. Write a love letter or a letter of complaint of 150 words to one of the above places.

5. Structure a long poem or piece of writing, dedicating a line, stanza, paragraph, or chapter to a selection of the above locations.

6. Use any of this material as groundwork for a fragment of childhood memoir, literary travel narrative, or poem.

7. For advanced students: chart itineraries through a deep map based on smells, colors, sounds, garbage, or shadows.

8. Create an imaginary town or neighborhood for a work of fiction. Identify several environments chosen from above for the setting of key scenes and sketch them out.

9. Class project for younger writers: make a deep map combining several sites and places, accompanied by drawings or photographs. This also makes for an interesting scrapbook or journal theme.

10. Write a postcard narrative from one of the above places such as a hospital, morgue, library, all-night café, prison, haunted house, pub.

11. Write a quest narrative using one of the above, for example, bus station, barbershop, funeral home, bookshop, Asian grocery.

12. Study the graffiti in a neighborhood and write about it. Or use graffiti as a structural element in a short piece of fiction. Combine graffiti with a postcard narrative.

13. Keep a street haunting diary for two weeks.

14. Visit several sacred sites in the area and write about the experience either as a *flâneur* or a pilgrim.

15. Combine a pilgrimage and a postcard narrative or deep map.

16. Organize some writing time in a few of the above locations, like a museum, art gallery, skating rink, train station, hardware store. See what stories are going on, what atmospheres intrigue you.

17. Write about getting locked in or lost in any of the above places.

18. Make a desire map of something that appeals to you and follow it. Write about your experience.

19. Find a cemetery that isn't for people and write about it (auto-demolition, pet cemetery, etc.).

20. Write about some curious place names you discover.

21. Take part in a collective event and write about it.

22. Write a travel essay about a religious or cultural festival as a pilgrim or *flâneur*.

23. Let yourself be inspired by the ideas of hypertime or deep travel and write a short essay.

---

[1] Mircea Eliade *The Sacred and Profane*, New York: Harcourt Brace, 1959, p. 24.

[2] Martin Gray, *Sacred Earth: Places of Peace and Power*, New York: Sterling Publishing, 2007, p. 11-12. Quoted by permission.

[3] Walter Benjamin, "The Return of the Flaneur," *Selected Writings 1927-1930*, Harvard U, Press, 2005, p. 264.

[4] Elizabeth Vander Schaaf, "Finding the Soul of the City," *Utne Reader*, September/October 1994.

[5] D.H. Lawrence, *Sea and Sardinia*, Cambridge: Cambridge University Press: 1997.

Chapter 3

The House of the Self

My House, Myself: The House as Symbol

The image of the house is perhaps one of the oldest and purest archetypal symbols of selfhood. Its verticality, linking sky and ground, speaks of our stratified consciousness. Its cellar plunges to the unconscious; its attic relegates the past to the castoff realm of memory. Its corridors and hallways guide us to the rooms where the substance of our daily lives is contained, nurtured, transformed. Moreover, it has a *face* of its own. The image of the archetypal house, standing alone among the elements, receiving the onslaughts of wind, rain, snow, hail, and human intervention, reflects our struggle for survival in the world.

According to French philosopher Gaston Bachelard (1884–1962), our feelings of safety, shelter, belonging, and repose are all connected to our earliest memories of domestic environments. In his philosophical study, *The Poetics of Space*, he investigates the symbolism of houses, rooms, and house furnishings in literature and in our lives. Bachelard believed that the act of daydreaming is a vital function of our psyche through which we may enjoy a deeper contact with ourselves and with the cosmos. In order to be free to daydream, however, we need to feel safe and at rest, and our feelings of safety and repose are bound up with our childhood memories of the houses and rooms where we felt safe and free to dream. Those memories in turn are related to our longing for an ideal house, and our attempts to create a real home for ourselves in adulthood. For Bachelard, our house is a sort of spatial poem.

> Home is a name, a word, it is a strong one; stronger than magician ever spoke, or spirit ever answered to.
>
> —*Charles Dickens*

He also suggests that the first domestic space we experienced is recorded in our memory through a series of forgotten reflexes and habits. Marcel Proust (1871–1922) develops a similar idea in the opening pages of Volume I, *Swann's Way*, in *Remembrance of Things Past* in which M, the narrator, in a state of semi-waking, relives sensations previously experienced in different moments of his life while the darkened space of his bedroom seems to whirl through time, transporting him to other rooms where he has fallen asleep and reawakened on several past occasions.

Writing Exercise: Reassemble a House From Your Past

Reconstruct a house from your childhood or more recent past by means of your bodily memory of it. Start with any detail that comes to mind. The "feel" of the stairs, steep or narrow;

the cold touch of a brass doorknob; the creaking of floorboards; the tingling of fresh air on your face as you opened your bedroom window in winter.

First, make an effort to call to mind those images that are *not* visual in order to create a framework. Then fill in the rest with visual detail. This exercise may be done in ten minutes, an hour, or over an extended period of time, filling a whole notebook. It can be done for hours, days, years.

The following may help you conjure up details.

> It is all in pieces inside me; here a room, there another, and here is a stretch of corridor that does not connect these two rooms, but is preserved all by itself, a fragment...
>
> —*R.M. Rilke*

❖ What smells or scents do you recall inside and outside?

❖ Do any textures stick in your mind: the nubby weave of a rug, peeling paint on a wall, a scratchy wool blanket, smooth wooden boards, greasy linoleum?

❖ What were your favorite places in the house?

❖ Were there areas you could not enter or ones that frightened you?

❖ Did you have a favorite hiding place? What did it feel like there?

❖ Examine the view from each of the windows. What could you see?

❖ Open a few doors from one room to the next. What did you find there?

⌒

Interiors

Kitchen

Memoirist and writing teacher Patricia Hampl often asks her students to describe their first kitchen. The kitchen is truly the vital center of our home, the place where natural elements are transformed through fire and water for our nourishment, where tradition meets our contemporary needs, and where exotic elements combine with the most ordinary and familiar. The kitchens of grandparents or older friends or relatives reflect traditions or simply "family ways" of doing things that may have forged our identities and influenced our habits in later life. Certain kitchen paraphernalia related to specific moments of the year or ritual celebrations may evoke joy or dismay, depending on how we felt about them.

Writing Exercise: Revisit a Kitchen

Choose one to work with:

- ❖ the first kitchen you recall from your childhood
- ❖ the first kitchen in the place where you lived as an adult, were first married or cohabiting with a significant other
- ❖ the kitchen of a house or apartment in a foreign country where you lived for a time
- ❖ the kitchen in a historical home you have visited

❖ a kitchen that gave you the feeling of abundance or poverty

❖ a kitchen you found cold and unwelcoming

❖ a kitchen where you prepared something special for someone special

❖ a kitchen where you felt overwhelmed by something you had to do there

Proceed as follows:

❖ Start with the floor. How was it patterned?

❖ Examine the stove, fridge, sink, and table, the walls and ceiling. What colors and materials dominate?

❖ Open drawers and cupboards. What's inside? Perhaps a forgotten object that meant something to you then?

❖ What was on the counters?

❖ Are there any time markers indicating the period or season, like clunky old toasters, glass milk bottles, fresh fruit or vegetables from a garden, holiday paraphernalia?

❖ What tools, equipment, or food were prominently displayed?

❖ Are any of those tools obsolete now?

❖ What smells do you remember, the pleasant and unpleasant?

❖ Taste the water in the tap.

❖ What did the window look out on?

❖ Did any significant events in your life take place there? Did you cut your lip on a table edge, discover you were allergic to chocolate, taste your first oyster, or, perhaps, learn to tie your shoes?

Take ten minutes to jot down brief impressions. Then see yourself eating at the table, or preparing food for others. Evoke a meal you made or consumed that was prepared in this kitchen. What was on the table? A kitsch salt-shaker? Bottles of pills? A tablecloth used for special occasions, old plastic placemats, or flowers someone brought you? See yourself in the company of someone who shared your life at that time. Remember a conversation at the table during a meal.

Write a narrative fragment of 300–500 words describing the meal and your relationship with the person, including bits of dialogue in your fragment.

Writing Exercise: Revisit a Bedroom

We really do spend a great deal of our life in this room. Proust's descriptions of his bedrooms are probably unmatched in the history of world literature, except for those of Xavier De Maistre (1763 -1821), a French writer and soldier who dedicated two entire volumes to describing his. Recall any bedroom from your past, though a childhood bedroom may work best for some.

Evoke any of the following:

❖ the feel and smell of the mattress, sheets, pillows, blankets

❖ the sensation of pitch darkness around your body

❖ how the dawn, moonlight, or streetlight shone into the room

❖ sounds you could hear in the middle of the night or upon waking

❖ the sound of wind, rain, or thunder, the silence of snow or fog

❖ noises that frightened or disturbed you

❖ the presence of another body, human or animal, in the bed or in the room

❖ sleeping naked or wearing socks or a hat to bed

- ❖ bed warmers or bedpans
- ❖ wetting the bed or sleepwalking
- ❖ getting out of bed on a freezing morning
- ❖ sweating all night in sweltering weather
- ❖ getting up way before dawn
- ❖ waking up and finding yourself inexplicably alone or in company
- ❖ waking up and finding yourself in an unexpected place or position
- ❖ a night of insomnia, illness, vivid dreams, or fear
- ❖ a night light, bedroom curtain, or ceiling fan
- ❖ being rudely or gently awakened in the middle of the night
- ❖ something hidden under the bed or mattress
- ❖ you or someone else hiding under the bed
- ❖ something on the bedside table
- ❖ the sensation of your body, your eyes, and eyelids upon waking
- ❖ the sensation of your feet on the floor or rug when you stand up from the bed

Use any of the above to create a memoir fragment or prose poem. For fiction writers, use any of the above to create a scene on the theme of going to sleep or waking up.

Writing Exercise: My Father's House Has Many Rooms

Choose one or more from the following list to work with:

- a room where books, toys, guns, hats, or liquor were kept
- a room with a distinctive smell
- a room where an animal lived
- a room where you or someone else played music
- a room where you made love in an unusual place
- a room where you quarreled bitterly with someone
- a room where you injured yourself or someone else
- a guest room, empty or occupied
- a room that was off limits or taboo, a room with a secret
- a room with a special view, intriguing door, or mirror
- a pantry or cellar where food was stored
- a sickroom or a room where a death occurred
- a room where something valuable was kept locked away or hidden
- a storeroom, attic, basement, or crawl space
- a room where you were locked in, on purpose or by mistake
- a room where something foreign was kept

Write freely for ten minutes, attempting first to "raise the ghost" through bodily memory using all the senses. Draw or sketch a map of the house and the room to prod your memory, then write a short descriptive, lyric piece or narrative prose passage. Use this material to create longer memoirs.

The exercise above is designed to trigger physical memories of environments in your home, but could also apply to other locations, including public places, like libraries or schoolrooms.

Writing Exercise: Uncomfortable Places

I can still recall the fear I felt as a child while standing at the top of a dark flight of cement stairs leading down into a neighbor's basement. The dim light bulb on the landing, the steepness of the stairs, the musky odor of earth from below all filled me with dread. The apprehension I felt remained with me for many years.

Some people develop phobias of certain places, like stairs, subways, or enclosed spaces, from some early trauma. Elevators, attics, closets are other places that make people and sometimes animals uneasy or fearful. Think of a place that made you apprehensive. Give yourself twenty minutes to do this exercise. Don't hold back and don't censor what comes.

Fiction writers: Write about a character suffering from a phobia connected to a place.

Writing Exercise: Workrooms

Was there a workshop in your house, a carpenter's bench with tools kept in perfect order, a sewing room with mannequins and bolts of cloth, a painting studio, a garage where you or your dad tinkered with cars, tools, or electronics? Did someone at home practice a trade or handicraft? What role did this activity have in the family economy? Was it tidy or disorderly?

How were the tools of the trade displayed? How did you feel about this room and what took place there? Were you allowed to help or made to keep a distance? How did this activity shape your personality or your imagination?

Describe the room and its contents. Try to recapture the atmosphere when a project was in process. Re-evoke an episode in 300 words.

Writing Exercise: Your Bathroom

And don't forget the bathroom, that necessary space connecting us to the greater elements of water and earth, a place of regeneration, purification, relaxation. An excellent setting for a sex scene, domestic confrontation; for solitary soul-searching, self-discovery, self-comforting, suicide, and of course, in detective fiction, murder. Think of all those lifesaving or potentially life-threatening substances in the medicine cabinet, the makeup with which we disguise ourselves daily, the cold mirrors and vanity lights.

Write 300 words about something unusual you once did in a bathroom.

Write 200–300 words about a daily ritual performed in the bathroom.

Narrate an episode that involves the loss or sight of blood in the bathroom.

Write about a perfume bottle that belonged to your mother.

Or look in your medicine cabinet, select three items, and connect them in a short story of up to 1,000 words.

Writing Exercise: Old Photos/Old Houses

Nothing is more melancholy than finding the photo of a house we once lived in, years ago, now vanished. Find a photo of the interior or exterior of a place where you once lived. Do you remember the day the photo was taken? Try to recreate the atmosphere in a short text of up to 300 words. You might begin "That day you/we/I..." Write about what can't be seen in the photo, or what has been left out.

Writing Exercise: Openings

Imagine opening a door, window, closet, drawer, suitcase, package, letter, purse, or book in a place where you once lived. Be surprised by what you find. Describe all the sensations of opening and discovery: keys, latches, fastenings, the gesture of opening, the smell inside. Write a short passage of 150 words.

House Furnishings

In her novel *Villette*, Charlotte Brontë (1816–1855) used spatial imagery, from landscapes to houses, schools, rooms, and even drawers and chests as symbols of the heroine's developing consciousness and transformation through time from a lonely orphan to a fulfilled and independent adult, integrated into the society of the foreign country she had adopted as her home.

Writing about her childhood in her memoir *Moments of Being*, published posthumously in 1976, Virginia Woolf

(1882–1941) used house furnishings as a framing device to organize her material. In her descriptions of daily life at home, the tea table, "fertilized" by young beauties and haunted by eccentric old men, became a microcosm of upper class intellectual life in Victorian society. Double doors, effectively separating private areas of the house from public ones, clearly delineated the hypocrisy and double standards of class-bound British society.

It has been said that whereas houses and rooms may represent the Self, our furniture represents our feelings and life functions. Gaston Bachelard argues that wardrobes, shelves, drawers, and chests are organs of our inner life. Investigate a piece of *your* furniture from this point of view.

Writing Exercise: Furniture

Choose a piece of furniture from your current home or from some past setting. Doors, tables, cupboards, bookcases, armchairs, and sofas lend themselves to this exercise.

Write for ten minutes, free associating. What function does this piece of wood, metal, cloth, or glass fulfill in family life? Does it unite or separate, hide or conceal, offer comfort or provide restraint? What emotions are evoked as you write? What events do you remember connected to it? Try to build a scene around the item you have chosen. Or tell a story in which it plays an important role.

Suggested Techniques For All the Above Exercises

Use one (or a mix of) the following techniques to describe a favorite place:

❖ Compile a list of objects, feelings, events, and sense perceptions clustered around a specific room or one or two selected pieces of furniture or furnishings

❖ Write a narrative of habitual events (i.e. routine) in a specific place, interlaced with brief mention of objects

❖ Focus on a specific feature of a house or garden (window, door, table, cupboard, closet, bed). Describe it, creating a mood only from the description.

❖ Recall an episode or create a scene centering upon a piece of furniture.

A World in a Room

To write about an exotic place, we needn't travel far. We may start with something as close by and familiar as the very room where we sit writing—or even the desk where we are working, which can provide more fascinating material than we imagine. This was the idea of Xavier De Maistre, who was confined to his room for forty-two days as a punishment for engaging in duels. To keep himself occupied, De Maistre set out to write an exploration of his bedroom entitled, *A Journey Around My Room* (1794) later followed by *Nocturnal Expedition Around My Room* (1825). His purpose was to examine his environment and describe ordinary objects as if they were being seen for the first time. In these two essays, he reflects on the history, function, and role in his life of his bedroom furnishings—bed, desk, bookshelves, pictures, and upon the general philosophical questions that such reflection called to his mind.[1]

In a bed we enter the world, and in a bed we die. It is a stage whereupon mankind perform by turns, amusing comedies, laughable farces, horror awakening tragedies. It is a cradle wreathed with flowers, it is the crown of Cupid, it is a sepulcher.[2]

De Maistre's point is that the humblest object contains a transcendent dimension—a belief shared by many other writers, from the English Metaphysical poets to French writers Marcel Proust and Francis Ponge. To perceive this dimension in our everyday environment we must find ways of looking at it anew. We must make the familiar strange. Writers as diverse as William Wordsworth, Samuel Taylor Coleridge, Arthur Rimbaud, and T.S. Eliot have wrestled with this problem, concluding that in order to achieve a more complete vision of our environment, we must bring to it a more vivifying form of attention.

In Alexander Pope's (1688–1744) mock-heroic epic poem, *The Rape of the Lock* (1712–1714), there is an exquisite scene in which the heroine, Belinda, dresses before going out to the card game where a lock of her hair will be cut by Lord Petrie. The objects assembled on her lavish dressing table—cosmetics, creams, powders, silver implements, and tortoise shell combs, have been brought to her boudoir through the power of English naval trade. The entire world resides in her room and nourishes her beauty. What was true of Belinda's boudoir is certainly true of our own homes nowadays, where some of the objects surrounding us have probably come from very far away. Some have come down to us from remote periods of history, others may just have come into being yesterday; some are made by hand, others mass-produced. Some are made of materials from exotic places or materials that have developed through the ponderous processes of nature: volcanic, erosive, and evolutionary.

Chairs, desks, tables, and beds provide the essential support to our daily lives, and have witnessed hundreds of "events" in which they too were protagonists. Handmade rugs and other items have their own romance.

Writing Exercise: Journey Around Your Room

American poet Louise Bogan's autobiographical essay: "Journey Around My Room" (1933) probably owes much to De Maistre. Here too, she departs from a description of the bed to describe her room, its furnishings and its situation within Manhattan, then reaches back to tell the story of the long journey from childhood that led her to New York.

Write a detailed description of a room in your home or elsewhere that holds specific significance for you. Tell the story of how you got there.

Suggested Reading

Louise Bogan, "Journey Around My Room"
Xavier De Maistre, *Journey Around My Room*

Knickknacks, Shrines, and Talismans

Writing Exercise: Your Knickknacks

In her essay "Street Haunting," Virginia Woolf discusses how our rooms and the objects collected in them are stamped with our personality and charged with memories. From the china bowl on her mantelpiece up swirls a cloud of associations mingling people, places, and chance encounters of her recent holiday in Italy. Investigate the contents and furnishings of your room from this perspective. What do your possessions say about you? Pay attention to those that have more symbolic or aesthetic value than practical: the seashells you keep in your bathroom, the bronze camel statuette on your dresser, the tiny globe pencil sharpener you have had since fifth-grade. What stories do they have to tell? What memories do they hold?

Focus on one object or make a selection and write 50 words per piece.

Or choose a knickknack connected to a humorous episode or one connected to a remote or almost forgotten time of your life.

For fiction writers: describe a character's personality through the objects kept in a drawer of a desk or bedside table, or for a woman, in her purse.

Writing Exercise: Personal Shrines

Bruce Chatwin begins his travel book *In Patagonia* with a description of a cupboard of knickknacks—a family shrine of sorts containing curios and odd objects, including what was supposedly, according to a family legend, "a piece of Brontosaurus." His childhood fascination for this shred of dried skin tufted with coarse hair and for the story of how it had come into his family inspired his future endeavors as a traveler and writer in search of the true origins of his "brontosaurus." Was there such a "shrine," curio cabinet, or reliquary in your childhood— in your own home, a neighbor's home, a school, church, or museum? Focus on a detail concerning it and write a passage about it.

Writing Exercise: Collections

Are you or have you ever been a collector of stamps, butterflies, Barbie dolls, knives, or old perfume bottles? Some psychologists believe that the passion for possessing stems from our need to feel complete. Others liken collecting to a sort of ritual worship of the objects themselves. What does your collection say about you? Are there pieces connected to specific places? Write 200 words about a prize piece in your collection.

Or describe a room in your home or elsewhere, a museum, for example, where a collection is on display.

Collecting is a distant kin of hoarding. For fiction writers: create a character and define his personality through the things he hoards.

Writing Exercise: Your *Lares*

The *Lares* were the household gods to whom each Roman household dedicated a shrine. We sometimes create shrines without quite realizing what they are. A shrine is a container for the soul of place, for our interior life, for treasured memories. Your *Lares* shrine might be a shelf or album with family photos. It may be a drawer with seashells or rocks picked up on a fondly remembered vacation. It may be a box of letters and postcards you feel particularly attached to, or a table where you keep objects of special meaning for you, or a place in your garden where you like to be alone. Returning to these objects or places, looking at them, arranging them, putting them back into order can be a restorative ritual. Is there such a shrine in your house, room, desk, or garden?

> We bring our Lares with us.
>
> —*Old Roman saying*

Deconstruct it piece by piece, then create a narrative or poem around each piece.

Writing Exercise: Stones

Some people can't resist picking up pebbles from along a beach or country road. One of my writing students collected stones as a child. She would stuff them into her purse and drag them to school, though they weighed heavy on her frail wrist. Her father, amused but puzzled, tried unsuccessfully to break her of this habit by removing them surreptitiously from her purse, which made her furious. Stone-gathering continued to be an obsession for her, as the huge collection strewn about her garden now reveals. In class she used memories of that stone-packed handbag to build a poignant memoir about her father.

Are there any memories connected to rocks or stones, pleasant or painful, in your early life? Do you have any stones or pebbles hidden away in drawers or bookshelves? If so, choose one that appeals to you particularly. Hold it in your hand for a while and ask yourself these questions. How did it come into being? Where did you get it? How does it evoke its place of origin? How does it react to the warmth of your hand? Imagine its interior as a hollow, habitable space. What would it be like to go inside there? What might you find inside? Where will it be when you are gone?

Writing Exercise: Domestic Objects

Take a domestic item that plays a role in your daily life, but which you have never really considered as material for your writing. Some suggestions: coffee pot, tea kettle, alarm clock, ironing board, car key, frying pan, telephone, eyeglasses, children's toy, dog leash, or an item of clothing. It should be something connected to a daily activity. What metaphorical power does it possess? Construct a poem, memoir passage, prose poem or short narrative around it.

Talismans of Place

An old tin kerosene lantern sits on a window ledge in the courtyard that sometimes serves as my writing studio in summer. Rescued from the attic of my husband's childhood home, scrubbed free of rust, it has been refurbished with a new wick and kerosene. I cannot guess what domestic scenes this lantern may have illuminated nearly seventy years ago, in wartime, in the Neapolitan countryside as explosions from Allied bombs racked the countryside, and my husband's mother, then a young girl, huddled by a wood-burning stove, mending socks for her stepbrothers. But it links me to a much more recent time, to a specific moment in my own life, when a lantern just like this one was my only source of light on summer nights.

On Crete, in a village with no electricity, I used a lantern like this to light my way home at night from the *kafeneon*, the village tavern and café, along a narrow path skirting the edge of the sea, then up a narrow staircase to a friend's tiny book-lined studio where fishnets and scuba equipment were stored, and drinking water kept in a tall, clay vase. There, lying on a prickly mattress stuffed with straw, I read by lamplight till late— literally burning the midnight oil. Whenever I light my husband's lantern now, the smell of kerosene brings back the atmosphere of that little room in Crete, the odor of musty books and brine, the sound of the waves, and the yellow sphere of the lantern's light, a cocoon in the darkness. Like a bottle with a genie, this object encapsulates the romance of not just a summer, but an entire phase of my life. It's a talisman of place.

Returning home, tourists and travelers usually bring something back with them—a token or trace of the place they have visited, if only a postcard or a photograph. According to writer and philosopher John Ruskin, our desire to photograph, make sketches, or buy postcards of places we visit originates in our instinct to possess what we consider beautiful. Souvenirs of our journeys function much in the same way: they preserve a spark from which to kindle a more complete memory or impression; they contain a germ of the soul of place.

The little Eiffel tower dangling on my keychain conjures up memories of the day I bought it—a bright, bitter cold November day outside the cathedral of Notre Dame as I stood on a medallion in the pavement from which all distances in France are measured, the symbolic heart of the city and of France itself, and then purchased a handful of Eiffel tower charms from a Russian street vendor wearing a tattered astrakhan hat and huge overcoat that smelled overwhelmingly of mothballs and wood smoke. Emblem of a city and fragment of my personal story, this cheap, insignificant object contains the seed of a past experience and the gleams of that autumn day.

Pilgrims to Lourdes or Lhasa leave votive offerings near altars or shrines once they reach their destination, little bits of themselves, and when they return home, take away tokens of the holy place: a vial of water from the healing well, a postcard of a saint, a bit of earth scraped from the sacred ground they have walked on to be preserved in a reliquary—or in the case of Tibetans, to be eaten. These talismans and amulets compress a moment of experience imbued with a sense of the sacred.

Among the objects you may have brought back from a trip (or perhaps received as gifts or heirlooms, or otherwise accumulated), some will be saturated with special meaning. Charged with sensations, emotions, impressions, desires, they contain a few particles of the energy of the place, person, or time to which they pertain. Through the principle of "sympathetic magic" ("like produces like") they allow that power to work upon our imagination even at a distance in time and space. The objects in our lives brim with life-stories, suggests Alexandra Johnson in *Leaving a Trace*.[3] Marcel Proust would surely have agreed, as we may note in the overture of *Swann's Way:*

I find quite reasonable the Celtic belief that the souls of those we have lost remain captive in some inferior being or animal, a plant, an inanimate thing, quite oblivious to us until the day, which for many never comes, when we pass by the tree or come into possession of the object in which they are held prisoner. Then they start and shudder, call out to us, and since we have recognized them, the spell is broken, now that we have delivered them they return to live among us. Thus it is with our past. All efforts of our intellect are futile. It is hidden beyond the realm and reach of intellect, in some material object and in the sensation which that object gives us which we do not suspect.[4]

Writing Exercise: Talismans of Place

Significant objects have stories to tell, emotions and sensations to return to us, but habit erases their evocative power. All it takes is a gentle interrogation to release the memories and stories they contain.

A word of caution: Talisman exercises may unlock powerful emotions. So be forewarned if you intend to use them in a classroom situation.

Look around your home, your desk—or poke about in your purse or wallet to discover a talisman. It may be a subway ticket from a city you visited some time ago, which you haven't thrown away, a bottle cap, a pebble. Or it may be something related to family life: a teapot that once belonged to your mother, a signet ring your uncle used to wear. Weigh the object in your hand as you reflect. What scenes, memories, feelings does it evoke? If nothing comes to mind as you examine it, see if any of the questions below offer interesting angles as you contemplate your object.

* ❖ Where was it originally made? Who made it? What was its function?

* ❖ What other things, people, needs, or experiences are related to it?

* ❖ Did it belong to someone else before? Where did you get it?

* ❖ Why does it appeal to you?

* ❖ In what ways could it be a metaphor, symbol, or time-marker in your life?

* ❖ If you were to lose it, how would you feel? Could it be replaced?

Write 300 words about it, using any of the considerations above. Or write 300 words about a private ritual involving your talismanic object.

For fiction writers: Write a scene about the loss, recovery, or transference of a talisman to another person.

Writing Exercise: Keys

As a child I was fascinated by the shape of skeleton keys and would sometimes buy them at the hardware store, although there were no doors in my parents' modern split-level suburban house that could be unlocked by such keys. When I moved to Italy and began exploring the rural areas of Tuscany and Tuscia, I was surprised to see that some of the old houses and doors still retained antique, iron keys of that same shape, handmade by blacksmiths, which looked as though they might have been passed down from the middle ages. Keys accumulate in my desk drawers and handbags—even when they are no longer needed, I somehow can't bring myself to throw them away.

Find an old key you haven't used for years. Clutch it in your hand and close your eyes. Imagine the lock into which it once fit. Was it the lock of a door, car ignition, drawer, safe, trunk, padlock, diary, suitcase? Recall as vividly as possible the "feel" of the door, box, drawer, and the context of which it was part. Turn the key in the lock and open it. Recall the physical gesture of turning and opening. Consider the many times you may have performed that gesture in the past. What do you find inside? What did it *smell* like inside the drawer/room/ box/ whatever? Dedicate ten minutes to writing a short passage. Then use the material for a story, lyric essay, or prose poem.

Writing Exercise: Imaginary Keys

If you can't find any old keys that you feel are suitable for the previous exercise, try doing it with an imaginary key to:

❖ the first door you remember locking all by yourself

❖ the first place you lived as an adult

❖ the first car you drove or owned

❖ something always kept locked in your house when you were a child

❖ something you keep locked now

Or write about a key you lost and never found again. Who or what was locked in or out?

Other objects suitable for this exercise can be: fountain pens, eyeglasses, wrist watches, foreign coins, pocket knives, old shoes, sports equipment, jewelry, rings—the important thing is that the object you choose should be something you haven't used or touched in a long time.

Writing Exercise: Lost Treasures

Sometimes our talisman may be something irreparably lost: a ring that slipped down the drain, a pair of eyeglasses fallen into the sea, a pot smashed to pieces, a photograph stolen along with your wallet when you were pickpocketed on a bus. It's the poignancy of being lost, irreplaceable, or irretrievable that makes the object so much more meaningful to us.

> Somewhere, those poor old things must still be knocking about.
> —*Constantine Cavafy*

Remembering an object you have lost, ask yourself these questions:

❖ When did you first realize it was gone? What emotions are connected to its loss?

❖ What might the object or its loss symbolize in your life?

❖ Where might it be now?

❖ What transformations or journey might it have undertaken since leaving your possession?

❖ Imagine the impact of fire, water, rain, wind, time, or being buried in the ground upon your object.

❖ Imagine someone else using your lost treasure. How does that make you feel?

Use the above reflections as the basis for a free association passage, poem, memoir fragment about your lost object and about loss in general.

This works well also with lost articles of clothing like a favorite shirt, tie, or swimsuit that somehow disappeared.

Writing Exercise: Tools

One intriguing aspect of old houses is the tools and utensils you sometimes find, stuck away in cupboards or attics: copper kettles for boiling water, handmade nails, cast iron equipment for cooking on the hearth, rusty scythes. In a thirteenth-century house in Italy where I lived for a time, we found a rustic ladder made from the trunks of two slim trees, still robust and reliable after surely more than eighty years. Investigate an antiquated tool in your home or surroundings. What information does it give you about daily life in the past? When do you suppose was the last time it was employed for its original purpose? Could it still be used today?

If you can't find anything in your own home, visit a Shaker or colonial museum and examine displays related to tools and household equipment. Choose an object and consider the thoughts of the person who made it—what may have passed through their mind while creating it. Imagine someone using it. What skills or precautions were required? Was the job tedious, dangerous, or time-consuming? Build a scene around the tool in 300 words.

Or take a peek in your garage or tool shed to find something you haven't used for a while: snow-shovel, broken lawn-mower, old hoes or rakes, abandoned outboard motor. Connect it to an event or person in your past and write a 300-word narrative or portrait. Or explain in 200 words why you haven't thrown it away. Or write about something unusual you found in the garage.

DIY crafts these days are very popular, from more complex arts like weaving or carpentry to making your own soap or wine following some traditional method or a treasured family recipe. In an essay of up to 500 words, describe the experience of making something yourself from scratch in the "old way" and your satisfaction or lack of it with the result.

For fiction writers: write about a haunted garage.

Writing Exercise: The Charm of the Obsolete

For years, my husband's family kept an old shortwave radio in their living room—one on which they had followed the events of the Second World War—as a family relic, even when it no longer worked. Old radios, black dial telephones, manual type-writers, black-and-white television sets, wind-up alarm clocks, and floppy disks all evoke scenes of personal history and are linked to familiar but forgotten gestures, once daily habits, now submerged in our bodily memory. If there is such an object in your house, dedicate a few moments to considering:

❖ when and how it came into your house

❖ what it represented in your family or in your family's daily life when it arrived

❖   when and how it passed from use

❖   what replaced it

Then connect it with a moment in the past—a historical event or a personal one—and build a memoir or fiction fragment from it.

Writing Exercise: Smells

Bruce Chatwin described a room from his childhood as smelling "of church." With this succinct metaphor, he conjures the cool odor of stones, flowers on the altar, polished floors and wooden pews, candle wax or incense, the air not quite fresh. It is a subjective description, churches smell differently to different people, obviously, yet it conveys a mood most readers can understand. Marcel Proust took the opposite approach of using multiple adjectives: In one famous description, he employs no less than five to describe the "nondescript" smell of his quilt on a winter morning.

Helen Keller once defined smell as the "fallen angel" of our senses since we so often neglect the information it provides. Think back to places in your life that you remember particularly for their smell: pleasant, unpleasant, peculiar. The smell of the ocean through your window, mothballs in a trunk of old clothes and photographs, bacon sizzling in a frying pan on Sunday mornings, or maybe, burning toast. For me, one unforgettable odor was the smell of books upstairs in the public library on hot summer afternoons as I browsed for novels that would take me elsewhere. To refresh your memory of places, you might look back at an earlier exercise in this book, "My

Father's House Has Many Rooms," and choose three to five from the list. Using either multiple adjectives or a brief formula employing "of" or "like," describe the smell in each room.

Or return to the list of public places in the Final Projects section of the previous chapter, pick a few that are memorable because of their distinctive smell: a smoky pub or pool hall, public swimming pool, schoolroom, bakery, shoe repair shop, etc. and use the above approach to describing smells.

Or write a lyric essay about an important smell in your environment.

Writing Exercise: Neighbors and Intruders

The exercises here have focused on interiors and home environments shared with family and friends, but other beings may have occupied your space: neighbors, transients, and intruders, animal or human. Write a text of 300 words dealing with one of the following.

* ❖ an annoying or angry neighbor
* ❖ an intrusion or invasion of your private space
* ❖ an incident in which you spied on a neighbor or your neighbor spied on you
* ❖ an incident in which something was stolen from your home

Light and Shadows

A friend of mine from Venezuela used to tell stories of his childhood home in an old hacienda without electricity out in

the countryside. There were tales of sorcery—a favorite aunt was poisoned by a bouquet of flowers given to her by a rival in love—and stories of ghosts in the house. "Of course, all that ended when we got electricity," he said wistfully. "The ghosts vanished forever."

Years ago in Florence, down at the end of the street where I lived around the corner from Piazza Santo Spirito, there was a little building with a small plot of garden enclosed within tall walls. Nothing grew in that unkempt garden except scraggly money-trees, bushes with silvery disc-shaped pods, like silver dollars, which rattled when stirred by a breeze. But atop the gate crouched a small stone sphinx, carved of marble, tinged gray by car exhaust. You would barely notice her if you walked past in the day, but at night the streetlight cast an enormous shadow of this sculpture upon the adjacent building, so that it loomed huge, filling the entire wall with a distorted, eerie apparition. We used to walk down to the house on summer nights to admire the sphinx's shadow, and even tried to photograph it, though the result fails to capture the magic of its evanescent form. That same year, I was the occasional guest of someone who had an old farmhouse outside Florence without running water or electricity. Evenings around the table were lit by a kerosene lamp. I still can recall the impression of wine flasks, tea kettles, coffeepots, our own profiles mapping the rough white plaster walls, like some gigantic shadow puppet play. Those shadows added their own rich texture to our conversation.

Writing Exercise: Shadow Watching

Turn off the lights and examine your home by candlelight or moonlight. What changes in your perception? Describe the atmosphere in a short text of 200 words.

Take a walk on a bright afternoon or on a moonlit evening. Notice the shadows around you: your own shadow, those of other people, buildings, animals, trees, the shadows of planes passing overhead, of clouds drifting low. Note the textures of shadows cast by streetlights, moonlight, lamplight, candlelight, fluorescent lighting, and bright sunlight inside or outside. Write a passage inspired by the experience.

For fiction writers, turn a shadow into a character.

Ghosts

No discussion of the *genius loci* would be complete without some mention of ghosts. The word itself comes from *"gast,"* an Old English word for spirit or soul. All cultures have their tales of ghosts and spirits tied to places or buildings. In Western literature, the earliest known ghost story recorded by Pliny the Younger includes all the trappings of nineteenth-century classics: rattling chains, a phantom, and an old house where a man was murdered. Whether you believe ghosts are just hallucinations or perhaps manifestations of a mysterious energy that may be palpable to some individuals, you cannot deny that ghosts enliven some of the world's best-loved theater, fiction, and films. Henry James was a master of the ambiguous tale, like *The Turn of the Screw*, in which we never know whether the ghosts of Peter Quint and Miss Jessel were perceived by others or only by the governess-narrator who may or may not be mad. In other ghostly tales by James, ghosts and apparitions are actually fragmented selves of the characters. In *The Jolly Corner*, a man who has lived abroad returns home to find the ghost of himself still living in his old house and discovers with horror who he might have become had he never moved away. The ghost as double appears in several of his other tales as well.

Writing Exercise: A Ghost Tale

Take Henry James's suggestion and go back to an environment of your past and raise the ghost of yourself as you would have been had you remained in that place. Use prompts from the above exercises dealing with interiors to help stimulate your memory. Then write a story of 1,000–3,000 words.

~

Symbolic Interiors in Fiction

Critics have noted how houses and spatial imagery began to acquire greater symbolic value in the English novel over the eighteenth century.[5] In novels such as Samuel Richardson's *Clarissa,* Charles Dickens's *Great Expectations,* and Charlotte Brontë's *Villette,* imagery related to domestic space not only symbolizes social or class status, but is used to expresses the protagonists' inner worlds and personalities. The writers of the gothic novel, like Ann Radcliffe or Horace Walpole, pushed this further. In their writing, architectural, spatial, and landscape images become supreme metaphors for pathologies and obsessions.

Of the places presented in gothic novels, castles and convents are favorite settings. It is interesting to note how the positive, symbolic values of these two images, castle and convent—which in earlier periods of literary history represented culture, order, power, and above all, safety—were transformed into their opposite in the gothic novel, becoming places of betrayal, transgression, fear, violence, and death.

Set alone in bleak, barren, often cursed landscapes, gothic castles and convents are rarely described as having well-defined, functional rooms or furnishings. Rather, they seem to be a confusing tangle of corridors, passageways, stairways, cells, and attics where the heroine is always being chased up to the turret or down to the dungeon. Pursuit and escape drive the narrative forward and on every page, readers savor the sublime, mingling delight with horror. These oppressive interiors and surreal landscapes are akin to the realm of nightmares and are evocations of the unconscious mind. Some critics claim that the birth and success of the gothic novel was a response to the terrors of the French Revolution and its aftermath, for it expressed the anguish, fear, and fragility of human beings besieged by an evil from which no social order could protect them.

The gothic penchant for assigning negative symbolic value to landscapes and interiors, either as projections of the essential narrative conflict or as mirrors of a character's delusions or obsessions, influenced many later writers of fiction.

In this passage from *Wuthering Heights* by Emily Brontë, for example, the description of the house and its setting is not only a symbolic portrait of Heathcliff's personality, appearance, and essence, but also, in part, a metaphor for the basic conflict underlying the novel itself: the lack of reconciliation of self, nature, and society. The words in italics represent figurative language mirroring all these levels, suggesting deprivation, distortion, coldness, and harshness, yet also rugged power and the rude, physical strength necessary for survival in such an environment.

> *'Wuthering'* being a significant provincial adjective, descriptive of the atmospheric *tumult* to which its station is *exposed* in *stormy* weather. *Pure, bracing ventilation* they must have up there at all times, indeed: one may guess the *power* of the *north wind* blowing *over the edge,* by the *excessive slant* of a few *stunted* firs at the end of the house; and by a range of *gaunt thorns* all stretching their limbs one way, as if *craving alms of the sun.* Happily the architect had foresight to build it *strong*: the *narrow* windows are *deeply set* in the wall, and the corners defended with *large, jutting stones*. . .[6]

In this passage from Charlotte Brontë's *Villette*, the heroine Lucy Snowe, after fainting on the street, wakes up in a strange room in a strange house. The words in italics represent visual patterns in the room's decor:

> A carpet where *arabesques* of bright blue *relieved* a ground of shaded fawn; pale walls over which a slight but *endless garland* of forget-me-nots ran *mazed* and *bewildered* amongst *myriad* gold leaves and *tendrils*. A gilded mirror *filled up the space* between two windows...In this mirror, I saw myself, laid, not in bed, but on a sofa. I looked spectral...[7]

Here the *arabesques* on the rug and the *garlands and mazes* decorating the walls recall the figure of the labyrinth symbolizing Lucy's confusion and puzzlement. At the same time, they are associated with one of Burke's attributes of the sublime: ceaseless repetition.

Writing Exercise: A Symbolic Setting

Write a descriptive/narrative passage involving a scene in which the landscape or interior reflects the protagonist's (or your own) inner state.

~

The Objective Correlative

This famous phrase coined by modernist poet T.S. Eliot refers to a symbolic process through which the inner world of feelings and impressions comes to be associated with the outer world of objects and events. For Eliot, as for other modernists, the social and moral challenges ushered in by the twentieth century required that artists and writers seek new means and methods of expression in order to convey what they felt to be the new human condition: a discontinuous and fragmentary sense of the real, a rootlessness, and the collapse of a once shared value system shaped by centuries of tradition. Artists, alone but free, had to find a way to make sense of this shattered world, now reduced to a heap of broken images, and salvage what they could. The creation of a work of art could only begin with a very subjective collecting and sifting of fragmented personal experiences.

According to Eliot, that collecting and sifting was the very essence of poetry-making, as he suggests in two critical essays, "The Metaphysical Poets" and "Tradition and the Individual Talent." For Eliot, the poet's mind is constantly reassembling snatches of life, creating new wholes from experiences completely unrelated to each other, like falling in love, reading philosophy, or even overhearing the tapping of a typewriter or smelling the odor of food cooking.[8] The mind of an ordinary person experiences life as chaotic and fragmentary, but the poet's mind functions as a crucible where words, impressions, sensations, emotions, and images swirl together to make "new compounds,"[9] or new works of art, when conditions are right.

To create this new whole, some form of cohesion—of glue—was needed. That cohesion was given by a symbolic process Eliot called "the objective correlative," through which writers and artists link emotion to the physical world of things and situations. In another essay, "Hamlet and His Problems," Eliot defines the objective correlative as a set of objects, situations, or chains of events that will trigger a particular sensory experience in the spectator (or reader), allowing him to understand the character's emotion.[10] The objective correlative, which may be a thing, location, or event, allows a writer to convey emotion without stating it overtly or providing a description. It privileges "showing" over "telling," shuns sentimentality and seeks the understatement. It is also important to note the use of the word "set." In Eliot's definition, the objective correlative is presented as a series of factors working together to express emotions beneath the surface. Since the poet chooses not to state the link between emotion and object/situation directly, the reader sometimes must work harder to discover the connection between the two.

One writer who adopted the objective correlative in fiction to great effect was Ernest Hemingway, who sought to capture in his writing the "real thing," which he defined as a series of motions and facts that produce emotion.[11] Hemingway's *The Sun Also Rises* (1926) is sometimes studied as an example of consistent use of the objective correlative, which contributes to his spare, muscular style. Some examples from this novel include the imagery of empty and half-empty glasses, a waiter mopping off a table, and Jake, the impotent protagonist, pouring his drink down the sink, all articulating his disillusionment and frustration. Another often-cited example of Hemingway's use of the objective correlative is found in his story, "Soldier's Home" (1925) in the exchange between the main character, a wounded soldier, and his mother at the breakfast table. While she speaks of her prayers and concern for his mental state, he notices the bacon fat congealing on his plate, suggesting his self-disgust and dismal prospects.

Celebrated novelist and writing teacher John Gardner created a series of writing exercises focused on the objective correlative. One of those was to describe a scene viewed through the eyes of a character who has just learned that his son has met a violent death, but without mentioning exactly what has happened, or the word "death."[12] The emotion had to be conveyed exclusively through the description of the scene from the man's point of view.

Examine a poem or piece of fiction and attempt to identify an objective correlative, remembering that it may be an object/set of objects, event/chain of events, or a situation that conveys an emotion without describing it. The passages previously quoted in the section Symbolic Interiors are also examples of the objective correlative. Find other examples to study and see how they work.

Writing Exercise: The Objective Correlative in Memoir

Think back to a time when you were in the throes of a very strong emotion: anger, love, sadness, fear, wonder, remorse. Recall the setting and situation in which you felt the emotion. Describe your perceptions filtered through your emotion without actually stating what has happened or how you feel. Find objects or situations taking place in the setting that might serve as objective correlatives.

～

Bringing It All Together: Final Projects

1. Write a lyric essay of 1500 words about a house or other interior from your past.

2. Write a selection of prose poems on your talismans, keys, stones, lares, or collection pieces.

3. Write a piece of fiction in which a talisman of place or a collection piece functions as an objective correlative.

4. Write about a shrine in your house and a ritual you perform there in 300 words.

5. Write about the smell of a neighbor's house in 150 words.

6. Write about a day you moved, in or out, in 300 words.

7. Apply a deep map or mental map exercise to a house or several houses in a neighborhood.

8. Write about a writer's house or room you have seen in 1000 words.

9. Write about a haunted house in 1000 words. Describe the rooms as symbolic interiors.

10. Write a quest narrative connected to buying a house or looking for a place to live.

11. Write a "journey around your room" about your writing studio, kitchen, or bedroom.

12. Write about a bedroom as a symbolic interior.

13. Describe a room through its reflection in a mirror.

14. Write about an object in your house that has metaphorical meaning for you.

15. Write about a fear connected to a place at home.

16. Describe the soul of place of your house. In what room is it most clearly manifest?

17. Write about being locked in or lost in a domestic environment.

18. An Italian proverb says: Houses may hide things, but they don't steal: Write about something you lost at home that never turned up again. Tell the story of a lost piece of paper.

19. Write about opening the front door to find a surprise.

20. Write about a box, safe, trunk, or drawer containing something important.

21. Write about a stairway or an elevator.

22. Tell the story of how you came to live in your house.

23. Write about having your space or privacy violated.

24. Write a love letter or letter of complaint to a house in your past.

25. Write an essay on how a room or house has shaped your imagination.

1. For an intriguing enquiry into De Maistre's work and personality, see Alain de Botton, *The Art of Travel*, New York: Pantheon, 2002.

2. Xavier De Maistre, *Journey Round My Room Followed By A Nocturnal Expedition in the Same Regions*, Philadelphia: Carey, Lea, & Carey, 1829, p. 10-11.

3. Alexandra Johnson, *Leaving a Trace*, Boston: Little Brown & Co. 2002, p. 69.

4. Marcel Proust, *Du Côté de chez Swann*, Paris: Gallimard, 1917, p. 44. Translation by the author.

5. Francesca Saggini and Enrichetta Socio, *The House of Fiction: The Representations of the House from Defoe to Woolf*, Cambridge: Cambridge Scholars Publishing, 2012.

6. Emily Brontë, *Wuthering Heights*. New York: Harper Brothers, 1858, p. 4.

7. Charlotte Brontë, *Villette*, Leipzig: Bernard Tauchnitz, 1853, p. 238.

8. T.S. Eliot, "The Metaphysical Poets," *Selected Essays*, New York: Harcourt Brace 1950, p. 247.

9. T.S. Eliot, "Tradition and the Individual Talent," *Selected Essays*, New York: Harcourt Brace 1950, p. 8.

10. T.S. Eliot, "Hamlet and His Problems," Selected Essays, New York: Harcourt Brace 1950, p. 124.

11. Ernest Hemingway, *Death in the Afternoon*, New York: Simon and Schuster, 1932, p. 12.

12. John Gardner, *The Art of Fiction* New York: Knopf, 1984, p. 37.

CHAPTER 4

Eating the Soul of Place— Food Writing

Food is the prime human need, and much of human history has focused on food. Open your kitchen cupboard and investigate its contents. The flour, sugar, salt, coffee, tea, and spices you'll find there, all cheaply and easily obtained at any supermarket, were once luxuries to die for. Each has a complex and sometimes astonishing history. Our need and cravings for these substances through the centuries launched wars, revolutions, and continental migrations, maintained the slave trade and promoted world-changing navigational discoveries and technological breakthroughs. The stainless steel knives in your kitchen drawer, the pots and pans, the state-of-the-art appliances for cooking and preserving food, all have evolved from a shadowy era when our remote ancestors carved flint and obsidian tools to kill animals or used gourds smeared with clay as cooking vessels. The discovery of fire and agriculture, of why it was more advantageous to plant seeds rather than eat them, of how some seeds could be ground up to make flour which could then, through the addition of water and leavening, be transformed into bread: these were the technological leaps that made us human. They are all related to food.

The food products of a locale are a tangible manifestation of its soul of place, containing the quintessence of its climate, soil, geography, and of the human intervention upon it. By eating those products, we absorb the *genius loci* into our own bodies. It becomes part of us. Recipes, cooking techniques, and all the paraphernalia connected to the preparation, serving, sharing, and consuming of food also express the soul of place. From a psychological point of view, food is our connection with our mothers, with our most archaic identity as a newborn for whom the very first physical sensation as an independent being is hunger. Food and hunger define who we are. Consider also the role of various foods in religious practices, myths, and celebrations in which bread, wine, pomegranates, grains, mustard seeds, apples, rice, mushrooms, beer, corn, and grapes have held symbolic value. To write about food is to write about our evolution, our feelings, and our deepest identity, or as some might say, our soul.

The Development of Food Writing as a Literary Form

Although references to food and dining may be found in many works of literature throughout the ages, and cooking manuals and recipe compilations in book form go back to the days of the ancient Romans, food writing as we know it today developed in France in the nineteenth century. Its most famous early exponent was Jean Anthelme Brillat-Savarin (1755–1826), author of *The Physiology of Taste*. This work is a collection of meditations on the pleasures of the table, considered both as art and as science. In his short, eclectic essays, peppered with personal anecdotes, aphorisms, scientific explanations, and recipes, Brillat-Savarin covers a very wide range of subjects: the physiology of our senses; the process of digestion; obesity; sleep and dreams; truffles; turkeys; coffee; the chemistry of frying; and the proper way to make hot chocolate. These writings, which may owe something to Montaigne's *Essays*, are the precursors of the personal gastronomic essay made popular by M.F.K. Fisher (1908–1992) the pioneer of modern food writing who, incidentally, also translated Brillat-Savarin's groundbreaking work into English.

Brillat-Savarin's chief rival was Grimod La Reynière (1759–1837), an aristocrat who gained fame as the first reviewer of restaurants in Napoleonic Paris and was known for a macabre sense of humor (he once organized his own funeral banquet to see how many people would attend) and pungent reviewing style. Another key figure to mention here is the more modern Georges Auguste Escoffier (1846–1935), a great chef who contributed to the modernizing of French cooking methods, whose cookbooks and kitchen management manuals are still major reference works on the subject. These three writers represent three major strands of food writing as it has evolved into modern journalism: the informative essay with a personal touch, the review, and the recipe which includes descriptions of technique and discussion of ingredients.

Early twentieth-century Paris also gave the world another great writer concerned with food: the French novelist Marcel Proust (1871–1922). His great *roman-fleuve, Remembrance of Things Past*, contains numerous references to the display, preparation, and smell of food, the art of dining, and the physiology and psychology of taste. The most famous food-related moment in his work and, perhaps in all literature, is his description of eating madeleine cakes dipped in linden-flower tea, which occurs midway through the opening chapter of *Swann's Way*, the first volume of his monumental work. The experience triggers a total recall of the emotions and sensations from his childhood, unleashing a stream of involuntary memories that he compares to Japanese paper flowers suddenly unfolding in a bowl of water. M, the narrator, then goes on to inquire into how this miracle occurred, concluding:

> When nothing is left of the distant past, when beings are dead and objects destroyed, only the smell and taste of things remain, fragile yet enduring, unsubstantial yet persistent, more faithful, lingering like souls, remembering, waiting, hoping on the ruins of all the rest, bearing upon their almost impalpable droplets, the immense palace of memory.[1]

Proust's great achievement was to unlock and give form to this flux of forgotten impressions. In this process he discovered that smell and taste were linked to our most ancient and authentic memories. The narrator's tasting of the madeleine goes beyond a gourmet's celebration of flavor to express the alchemy of sensation, consciousness, and memory.

Since 1937, when M.F.K. Fisher published her first book, *Serve it Forth*, food writing has become one of the most popular, multifaceted, and ever-expanding forms of writing in the USA. From fiction focusing on food like Joanne Harris's *Chocolat* to memoirs of home-cooked meals prepared in kitchens all over the globe, we love to read about food as much as we love to eat it. Food bloggers are legion. Some have evolved into highly successful and lucrative brands, launching restaurants, food services, and magazines. There is even a journal dedicated exclusively to literary food writing, *Alimentum, The Literature of Food* (www.alimentumjournal.com) that features food fiction, essays, menu poems, and much more.

Below follows a list of a few older and recent classics of food writing memoirs.

Suggested Reading

Elizabeth Bard, *Lunch in Paris*
Julia Child, *My Life in France*
Fuchsia Dunlop, *Shark's Fin and Sichuan Pepper*
M.F.K. Fisher, *The Art of Eating*
M.F.K. Fisher, *How to Cook a Wolf*
Elizabeth Gilbert, *Eat, Pray, Love*
Adam Gopnik, *The Table Comes First*
David Lebovitz, *The Sweet Life of Paris*
Frances Mayes, *Under the Tuscan Sun*
Peter Mayle, *French Lessons: Adventures with Knife, Fork, and Corkscrew*
Ruth Reichl, *Garlic and Sapphires*

Bread

In one of the world's most ancient epic poems, the Sumerian *Epic of Gilgamesh*, the act of eating bread is the touchstone of humanness. Enkidu, the hairy, green, wild man and forest dweller destined to become the god–king Gilgamesh's companion of exploits, loses his ability to communicate with animals after tasting bread, and from that moment on becomes fully human. Elsewhere in the poem, loaves of bread are used to mark the passing of time while Gilgamesh sleeps, failing the test of wakefulness necessary to obtain immortality. The central role bread plays in many of the world's great religious scriptures, traditions, and ceremonies reveals the universal sacredness of this primary food. In the New Testament, bread and wheat are a major symbol of spiritual life. The petition in the Lord's Prayer, "Give us this day our daily bread," refers to much more than just the food necessary for our nourishment and physiological survival, claimed Pope Benedict XVI: it is the higher substance of the Holy Sacrament necessary for our soul.[2] The word *companion* derives from the Latin *com* (with) + *panis* (bread) and in some Eastern European traditions, guests are ritually greeted with bread and salt in sign of sacred hospitality. The vital role of bread is reflected also in the many metaphors to which it is connected: "staff of life" (support), "daily bread," "put bread on the table," "breadbasket," "bread and circuses," "bread and roses," and the almost universal usage of the word "bread" (or "dough")— from Cockney rhyming slang "bread and honey" to urban anywhere to signify "money."

Bread is also one of the world's most diversified staples. Traveling from continent to continent, you'll discover thousands of variations on the basic triad of flour, water, and yeast, obtained by using different types of flours ground in varied consistency from different grains, seeds, and tubers; different liquids like milk, beer, or broth, which may substitute water; additions of spices, herbs, seeds, eggs, or sugar; and different methods and types of leavening and baking. Aside from being baked in an oven, bread can be baked on coals or a sun-heated terracotta tile, or boiled in a tin can, or fried on the hood of a hot car. Even the type of wood burned in a wood oven may bring out a distinctive flavor in the bread. Bread dough is also a sculptural medium and may be shaped in myriad forms for ritual purposes. To study the bread and bread-making techniques of a country, town, village, or family is to study its history, religion, and customs.

Writing Exercise: Bread

Choose one of the following as the basis of a story, essay, poem:

- ❖ a ritual bread you have been offered and tasted
- ❖ buying a loaf of bread in your own neighborhood or in an unfamiliar one
- ❖ the experience and sensations of preparing and eating your own bread
- ❖ an unusual bread or an unusual use for bread
- ❖ sharing bread with a stranger
- ❖ a foreign bread
- ❖ a bread you can't buy anymore

Writing Exercise: Early Memories of Food

Proust's entire childhood rushed to his consciousness after he had nibbled a few soggy madeleine crumbs. Are there any foods that might work this magic for you? What are your earliest memories of food? One of my earliest food memories is the unpleasant tingle of Coca-Cola fizzing up my nose when I took my first sip. Here's my list of foods that evoke distant memories:

- Wonder Bread
- rice
- lemons
- pancakes
- oranges
- birthday cake
- champagne
- Coca-Cola
- coffee
- oysters

Now write your own. What associations surround your memory? What anecdotes do you recall?

Writing Exercise: Sensory Recall: Re-Evoking a Flavor

The following exercise should be done at least once in the exact order given, completing each phase. The more time you dedicate to it, the more interesting your results.

❖ In the first phase, find a color photograph, magazine ad, or reproduction of a painting portraying food that appeals to you. Fruit and vegetables make good choices for this exercise, but you could also use dairy products or even a cheeseburger or a glass of wine. After studying the picture, try to recall the exact smell and taste of the food and describe it using any means that seem appropriate. Describe your memory of it in up to 50 words.

❖ To proceed to the second phase, you'll need to have handy a real specimen of whatever food you have chosen. Taste it now and write down a description immediately afterwards. Be very free in your method of description. Put both descriptions away. NB: some people like to do the tasting phase blindfolded, which adds an extra dimension.

❖ Let some time lapse: ten minutes, a half hour, an afternoon, or twenty-four hours. The results may change according to your time interval. Find some quiet time for yourself. Sit down, close your eyes, and try to *recall* the exact taste and sensation of the food. Note down your impression in up to 50 words.

❖ Reflect on *why* you chose that particular food. Did tasting it or trying to recall its taste evoke any memories, sensations, or emotions? Make a note of these, if so.

❖ Lastly, gather all your notes from the three phases, compare them, and write a fourth piece incorporating data from each one.

This exercise may be applied to the sense of smell, following the exact same five phases. You could also adapt the same method to the other senses in recalling places, people's faces, objects, animals, etc.

Note: This exercise can also be compressed in a workshop session of an hour or so. The important thing is to pause between the second and third phase to clear the mind of previous impressions and suspend your judgment about what you think it *ought* to taste like.

Food Places

We often associate favorite foods with specific times and places: sun-ripened tomatoes from your garden, fresh trout from a stream, or a cup of steaming espresso sipped in a sunny café in Rome. Holidays also have their distinctive foods associated with family. Think of a time and place associated with a particular food and write a lyric essay of 1,000 words. You might choose from:

- a homegrown vegetable or fruit
- a food you gathered, captured, or hunted in the wild
- a food associated with a holiday celebration
- a food you stole
- a food associated with a person
- a food you were forced to eat

~

The Vocabulary of Food Description

A well-crafted food description, whether in a short story, travel essay, review, or memoir calls for writing so vivid that the reader participates in the total experience, compounded of flavor, smell, texture, sight and occasionally even the *sound* of food as it is served or eaten (tinkling ice, sizzling platters, crunchy celery) the physical sensations of the tongue, palate, and throat; as well as the atmosphere surrounding the experience of dining, including the expectation and anticipation of pleasure derived from food and the satisfaction—or disappointment—produced by a meal. Describing the taste of food is a special challenge to the writer in English, given that our language has fewer words for taste sensations than, say, French or Italian, and after all, there are only five basic tastes: sweet, sour, bitter, salty, and umami, although I would add pungent or piquant to the list. Below are some suggestions for enhancing your food descriptions.

First, take a look at the main categories for taste listed in *Roget's Thesaurus,* a timeless, indispensable reference, and for many writers, a source of inspiration. I recommend investing in a paperback copy to browse through slowly when researching a particular category of experiences or things. The digital edition is more compact and much more limited in word choices. It's good to use for finding a synonym quickly but not for ruminating on nuances of meaning.

As a subcategory of "Sensation" we find: "Taste"—"Insipidity"—"Pungency"—"Condiment"—"Savoriness"—"Unsavoriness"—"Sweetness"—"Sourness," with various references to other headings in other areas, such as "Uncooked" or "Tough." Interestingly, both "Bitter" and "Salty" fall under the category of "Pungency" and do not merit categories of their own. Also of note: one of the longest entries in the section deals with the taste of tobacco. Analyzing these categories and semantic groups, we will discover that food description hinges primarily on flavor, consistency, texture, temperature, physical and emotional reaction to taste, and manner of preparation. Here are some examples: For flavor: herby, peppery, gingery, gamy, nutty, smoky, fiery, mordant, earthy. For consistency: moist, dry, soggy, gooey, gummy, watery, slimy, lumpy, pasty, rubbery. For texture: grainy, frothy, flakey, puffy, leathery, crispy, stringy. For temperature: chilled, boiling, steaming, icy, lukewarm. For physical and emotional reaction: delectable, ambrosial, sickening, nauseating, yummy. For manner of preparation: fried, burned, charred, fricasseed, undercooked, undone. However, many excellent descriptions of food use words not generally related to food at all, such as metallic, papery, old socks, mud, or metaphorical references, including austere, honest, generous, revolutionary, sublime, volcanic, decadent, swirling.

Writing Exercise: Describe a Food

Take a food you love or hate and investigate the many adjectives or metaphors you may use for a complete description including dominant flavor, persistency of flavor, consistency, texture, temperature, physical and emotional reaction, and manner of preparation, without naming the food. Take ten to fifteen minutes to write your text, then read it to a friend and let them guess what it is.

Then find antonyms to create the exact opposite description. For example if you described a food like chocolate, coffee, or beer in pleasurable terms, try describing the same flavor, consistency, or texture as unpleasant or disgusting.

In 30 words or less, describe one of the basic tastes—sweet, sour, salty, bitter, umami, or piquant—without referring to food.

Describe the taste of a medicine or food that made you feel sick.

With other writers in a class or writing group, hold a food description contest in which everyone describes the same food.

Fiction writers: Sketch a character who has an aversion to a certain food. How would the character experience and describe it?

Writing Exercise: Strong Flavors

Choose from below. Taste and describe using metaphors or nonfood-related images in short passages of up to 25 words.

- ❖ olive oil
- ❖ fresh basil
- ❖ dill
- ❖ garlic
- ❖ tomatoes
- ❖ ginger
- ❖ lemon peel
- ❖ chocolate

- coffee
- green tea
- vinegar
- sage
- wine
- shrimp
- whiskey
- soy sauce
- sugar
- hot pepper
- green pepper
- black pepper
- cinnamon
- cloves
- curry
- smoke
- air
- skin
- tears
- seawater
- paper
- stone

❖ pencil

❖ your own lips and mouth

Writing Exercise: Forbidden Foods

Recreate the memory of a forbidden food—something you felt guilty about eating or drinking.

Writing Exercise: A Memorable Meal

One of the most delicious meals I have ever eaten consisted of bread just baked in a resurrected Tuscan wood oven, dribbled with olive oil, topped by a slab of tangy pecorino cheese bought from a shepherd who lived in a tower, accompanied by a glass of fine chianti I had spent an afternoon bottling with a friend, ending up with wine-soaked shoes in a cellar.

In 750–1,000 words, describe a memorable meal you had at home or on vacation, alone, or with family and friends. Recreate every detail from the table, overall setting, food, atmosphere.

Or write about an object that was always on the table in your house at dinnertime.

Writing Exercise: The Strangest Food You Have Eaten

In her essay, "Sourtoe Cocktail," published in *Her Fork in the Road*, an anthology of food and travel writing published by Travelers' Tales, the author, Diane Rigda, describes drinking a whiskey sour containing a grayish, pickled human toe. Have you ever had an encounter with a culturally alien food? If so, describe the experience in *all* its particulars.

Writing Exercise: Write a Recipe

Recipes offer rich material for storytelling, memoir, and poetry. One of the most famous recipes in literature is found in the witches' scene in MacBeth: *Double, double toil and trouble. . .* which in turn may have been inspired by the myth of the Celtic witch, Ceridwen. Every recipe contains multiple stories concerning people, places, and situations if you consider its origins, ingredients, and transmission to us through time. The ways ingredients are procured and recipes prepared, eaten, or shared all encode histories of families and communities. Techniques and times of preparation transmitted in a recipe can tell us a lot about domestic life and economic circumstances (not to mention the status of women) in the period in which it originated.

Use a recipe for the core of a poem, story, or travel essay. Aside from the aspects mentioned above, consider also the buying and selecting of the ingredients, a discussion of those ingredients, and what makes the recipe unique.

Writing Exercise: Food as Metaphor

In her extraordinary poem, "In Time Like Air," which owes much to the Metaphysical poets, May Sarton compares the dissolving of salt into water and its return to crystalized form through evaporation as a metaphor for losing one's identity when falling in love and then finding it again. Find a food that might be metaphorical for you and use it as the basis of a poem or lyric essay.

Writing Exercise: Food in Art and Poetry

Since the days of the ancient Romans and Etruscans, food has been a favorite subject for painters in the West. Cezanne's apples and Matisse's lemons find their forerunners in Pompeiian frescoes of figs, grapes, and bread. Poets like Wallace Stevens have used artworks depicting food as the subject of poetry; Edward Weston's famous photograph *Pepper* shows how sinuous and sexy even a vegetable can be. Find a photograph or reproduction of a painting or sculpture of food and use it for the basis of a meditation, essay, or poem.

"Object poetry" made popular by Francis Ponge takes a painterly approach to describing things, like sea shells, stones, and especially food, which involved close scrutiny of the object and detailed visual detail. Pablo Neruda instead sought to celebrate humble things in our daily lives, including fruit and vegetables, in his Odes. Read Ponge's "Oyster," Neruda's "Ode to the Lemon" and "Ode to the Tomato," and Erica Jong's *Fruits and Vegetables* for a variety of approaches to the poetry of food. Then choose one of the foods you have worked with in this chapter as the focus of a lyric essay, prose poem, or ode.

Synesthesia

Synesthesia is a neurological condition in which the activity of one sense merges with another. For example, the perception of hearing may trigger activity in the sense of sight. The phenomenon was first documented by John Locke, who recorded the case of a blind man who claimed he saw the color red whenever he heard the sound of a trumpet. In medical literature, individuals gifted with (or suffering from) involuntary synesthesia are called *synesthetes,* among whose ranks are counted a great number of artists, musicians, and composers, like the Russian abstract painter Wassily Kandinsky, who attempted to paint symphonies in colors and lines. Researchers have discovered that synesthesia is more common than once believed, and may involve a great variety of sensorial and emotional experiences. There are time-space synesthetes, who experience time as located in physical parts of their bodies; there are tactile-emotive synesthetes, who experience a specific emotion whenever they touch a certain texture like velvet, glass, or toothpaste. There are documented cases of stroke victims who can feel sounds and of individuals who can hear patterns produced by moving dots on a screen. New forms of synesthesia are being discovered all the time.

> And all who heard
> Should see them
> there . . .
>
> —*Samuel Taylor Coleridge*

Although examples of synesthesia appear in English Romantic poetry, it was the French symbolists, Charles Baudelaire and Arthur Rimbaud, who popularized this as a mode of poetic experience. Baudelaire's greatest synesthetic poem is "Correspondences," in which perfumes are compared to children's flesh, the color green, and the sound of oboes. Rimbaud's most famous synesthetic poem is *Vowels,* in which he assigned each vowel a color.

Synesthesia may be useful in describing smells, tastes, sounds, and physical sensations, using the language of one medium to describe the sensations of another. For example "a fragrant thought," "a yellow perfume," or "a purple scream."

Writing Exercise: Synesthesia

Revisit one of the exercises you have done in this chapter and apply a synesthetic approach to describing flavor and taste. Rewrite your passage in synesthetic images or create a new prose poem, story, or poem based on a synesthetic experience.

***

Eating Out

In 2002, Irish-American novelist Thomas E. Kennedy published a 400-page experiment entitled *Kerrigan's Copenhagen*,[3] combining an autobiographical novel with a guidebook to the city of Copenhagen. In the story, Kerrigan, an American expat writer, romps in picaresque style across the city, doing research for a book he is going to write about the bars and eateries of his adopted home. Accompanied by a seductive Research Assistant, Kerrigan leads the reader on a series of gourmet and erotic adventures, while offering a whirlwind introduction to the cultural history of this northern capital. Set in spring, the novel tells the story of autumnal lovers reawakening to the pleasures of life, which they discover chapter by chapter, street by street, and drink after drink as they research the city's many locales. The street addresses of the "real life" restaurants, bars, and cafes they visit are provided in the heading of each chapter so that readers can check them out personally on their next trip to Copenhagen. This tour de force is also the essence of *flânerie*.

Writing Exercises: Eating Out

I. Find a public eating place where you like the atmosphere and feel at home. Spend some time there with a notebook, and jot down impressions of the place, people, atmosphere, and food. Use your notes as a basis of a story or travel essay.

2. Create a scene with dialogue between two characters who come into conflict over the issue of food.

3. Write your own brief fiction/guidebook in which a character or narrator visits four or five locales in your hometown or a city you love. Consider also using the postcard narrative.

4. Research a food market (see the section Markets earlier in this book) or bakery, brewery, candy store, etc. and write a fictional scene taking place there.

❧

Bringing It All Together: Final Projects

1. Write a lyric essay combining the sensory recall exercise with synesthesia to describe a food or drink.

2. Write an essay or memoir linking one of the kitchen-related exercises in the previous chapter with a food writing exercise in this chapter.

3. Write a travel narrative in which food figures prominently.

4. Write a quest narrative involving food.

5. Write a myth about the origin of a food.

6. Go to the library to find an old cookbook from decades ago and select an unusual recipe that would be impossible or difficult to prepare today. What does it tell you about daily life back then? Use it as inspiration for an essay or story.

7. Follow a pizza, or any other favorite food, by making a deep map or desire map. Consider any of these: the production of its ingredients, preparation, distribution, delivery, consumption, enjoyment, waste.

8. Write about a sacred food or sacred meal. Or about food and transgression.

9. Write about the connection between a food and a place in your life.

10. Write about food and garbage.

11. Follow a vegan or vegetarian desire map.

12. Write about making/growing your own food connected to a domestic environment in your past.

13. Try a wine tasting experiment and write about it.

14. Write about a taste not connected to food in 300 words.

15. Write about an unpleasant food smell in a kitchen or cafeteria in 300 words.

16. Participate in a festival or collective event involving food and write about it.

17. Organize some writing time in a place where food is prepared, sold, or served.

18. Master a recipe for a dish you don't know how to make. Write about the experience.

19. Write a piece of fiction that weaves a recipe into the plot.

20. Write about going hungry in 300 words.

21. Write about a food that expresses the soul of place of your neighborhood or hometown in 300 words.

22. Set a piece of fiction in a dining room, diner, or restaurant.

23. Write about eating in a car or train.

24. Write about a meal you consumed in a hotel room or strange bedroom in 300 words.

25. Write about food you prepared out of doors.

26. Write about food as transformation.

27. Write about a spice or condiment in 300 words.

28. Write a series of prose poems or a postcard narrative connected to food items or food places.

29. Write about foods you avoid in 300 words.

30. Volunteer at a soup kitchen or other place where food is prepared and served free of charge. Write about the experience.

31. Write about an acquired taste.

32. Write about the taste of water in 300 words.

---

[1] Marcel Proust, *Du Côté de chez Swann*, Paris: Gallimard, 1917, p. 46. Translation by the author.

[2] Pope Benedict XVI, *Jesus of Nazareth*, Vatican City: Libreria Editrice Vaticana, 2007.

[3] Later revised as Thomas E. Kennedy, *Kerrigan in Copenhagen*, New York: Bloomsbury, 2013.

CHAPTER 5

Submerged Territories— Writing and the Unconscious

After a trip to Orvieto where he visited Etruscan sites, Sigmund Freud (1856–1939) had an odd dream: his wife gave him salty water to drink poured from an Etruscan funerary urn. On another occasion, he dreamed he was alive in an Etruscan tomb occupied by two skeletons. The intuitions he gained from reflecting on these dreams lay the foundation for his pioneering theory that dreams are a form of wish fulfillment, as he explains in *The Interpretation of Dreams* (1899). They had revealed to him how the unconscious mind dismantles and reassembles forgotten places, objects, and experiences of our waking life to send us oneiric messages about needs and desires of which we may be unaware. Freud had a very simple explanation for the first dream. He had become very thirsty while asleep so his mind tried to compensate, dreaming of water. The salty taste of funerary ashes in the water was strong enough to make him wake up and take a drink, alleviating his discomfort. The second dream was more complex. He believed it was fulfilling his desire to be immortal. Since the publication of Freud's groundbreaking study, theories and techniques for exploring our unconscious mind through dreams and free association have multiplied. Some methods related to the Jungian and Gestalt schools offer rich insights and practices writers may use to tap into their creativity. We'll be looking at a few in this chapter.

Freud's discovery that dreams may communicate information about our physical and emotional needs that is hidden from our conscious self was not a new idea. In the ancient Mediterranean, the interpretation of dreams was a highly refined medical practice carried out in special locations, such as the temple of Asclepius in Epidaurus, where incubation was performed. In this rite, the patient underwent a phase of purification and then slept in the temple to receive a dream. In the morning, the priest interpreted the dream to discover the origins of the patient's illness as well as the course of treatment required to cure it. The popular belief that "night brings counsel," that if you "sleep on" a problem, you'll find a solution, is a vestige of this age-old ritual.

Similar beliefs are found all over the world, from the American Southwest to Africa and Australia, where certain places are thought to have the power to influence dreams, bringing messages or prophecies from the gods or ancestors, revealing secrets, or offering medical or spiritual advice. In Sardinia, where a form of shamanism underlies many peasant traditions, it was customary even in relatively modern times for peasant women to sleep in prehistoric sacred sites or caves in order to dream of future husbands or enhance fertility in some way. The Tibetan scholar Evans-Wentz found similar traditions still alive in rural Ireland in the early twentieth century. These practices suggest that there is a creative collaboration between our environment and ourselves ceaselessly taking place at a subliminal level. What we are dealing with here, the ancient Romans might say, are the mysterious workings of the *genius loci*.

Writing Exercise: Dream Places

Freud distinguished between dreams influenced by immediate stimuli, like thirst, indigestion, or temperatures of heat and cold, and those by deeper psychological factors. Have you ever had a dream that might have been influenced by your environment in any way? Consider both physical factors like an uncomfortable mattress or disturbing noise and emotional ones like feeling ill at ease in an unfamiliar room or snug and safe in a familiar one. Write a short text of 300 words about sleeping and dreaming in that place.

Fiction writers: Reread the section on "Symbolic Interiors" and write a short scene in which a dreamer, a dream, and a setting mirror each other.

Writing Exercise:
Working with Spatial Imagery in Dreams

As William Least Heat-Moon suggests in *PrairyErth*, our deepest and most authentic connection to a place may be revealed when we dream about it. Are there environments that reappear in your dreams? Rooms, houses, streets, roads? I often dream of my parents' house—the basement door, the kitchen window, the backyard fence, although only a few details are recognizable.

The rest is a collage of unknown rooms and impossible stairs. I also have recurring dreams of the sea, not an easily accessible beach, but vertical walls of sand dropping straight down into unquiet water.

Examine your dreams to see if there are repeating spatial patterns, landscapes, architectural elements or details. Then, choose a spatial image from a dream and try this exercise in three phases that draws inspiration from Gestalt dream therapy in which the patient converses with objects or people appearing in dreams.

Phase I: Take ten minutes to write down as much of the dream as you recall. Then concentrate on the particular image, like a door, room, window, gate, etc. you want to write about. First, in up to 50 words, write a physical description of the place/object. Next, in a shorter passage, describe the emotions or feelings the place evokes in you. If any proper names of people or places pop into your head, write them down.

Phase 2: Find an object that might represent the image: it could be a shoebox, a chair, or a rough sketch on a piece of paper. Place the object or sketch before you, as if sitting face to face with a friend or interlocutor. You are now going to have a conversation with your image, out loud or on paper. Ask it a question. If no question pops into your mind, try one of these.

Who are you?

Where do you come from?

What do you see?

What do you know?

Why are you here?

Give yourself up to twenty minutes to write the answer, using the first person, writing from the image's point of view.

Phase 3: Take a break, then go back to your desk and without reading your text, write a concluding line in the second person. Then reread all your texts in a sequence. Have you learned something about yourself?

The above exercise can be used with any type of image, not just spatial ones, in a dream, or a story, poem, or other text, or even with any objects and places encountered in waking life.

⌒

Dream Journaling

Many writers and creative thinkers have recorded the experience of receiving inspiration from their dreams, sometimes in the form of a cyphered language they had to interpret, other times in the form of revealed texts or images they were urged to record upon waking. This happened to the poet Coleridge after falling asleep while reading a historical account of Kubla Khan's summer palace in Xanadu. In his dream, he saw the text of a 300-line poem. Upon waking, he started writing it down, but was unfortunately interrupted by a visitor. When he finally managed to get rid of the unwanted guest and go back to his poem, he found he had forgotten the rest. The haunting fragment he had preserved was "Kubla Khan," a masterpiece of English poetry.

Robert Louis Stevenson, the Victorian author of adventure and gothic-tinged tales, also sought inspiration from dreams. In his memoir, *Across the Plains,* he recounts how he drew scenes and landscapes from his dreams for *Doctor Jekyll and Mr. Hyde* and explains a method of self-suggestion to stimulate dream activity. Some writers have used such techniques to initiate their writing process, from Katherine Mansfield, who conceived stories while lying in bed with her left hand pressed to her temple to Stephen King, who recommends committing to a routine of daydreaming and writing which he calls "creative sleep." King also claims that while recuperating from his injuries after being hit by a minivan, he had very intense dreams about four men in a hut in the woods, which evolved into his novel *Dreamcatcher.*

Dreams can provide content, imagery, ideas, stories, characters, symbols, moods, or simply unblock creative energies. To transform the rich, raw materials they provide into a reusable resource, consider keeping a dream journal for a period of time. If you have never done that, here are a few tips for getting started.

Before You Start: Preparing to Dream

Physicists often refer to the "observer effect" through which the act of observing a phenomenon influences the outcome of the process under observation. The same thing happens with dreams. Research has shown that the intention of remembering or working with dreams may alter our dreaming process, causing our dreams to assume specific patterns or forms depending on the school of interpretation being applied to the dream.

Dreams, then, respond to conscious and unconscious suggestion. In antiquity, when dreams were used for divination, rites of purification were performed before dreaming to make sure that during incubation the dream would come from the gods, i.e., a higher level of consciousness, and not from immediate physical stimuli. If you are going to be delving into your dreams, try creating a ritual of your own to predispose your mind toward the dreaming process.

Some people find it helpful to take a relaxing bath, listen to music, meditate, read inspirational texts, glance through picture books or at other images to engage the dreaming self. Before going to sleep, suggest to yourself that you would like to dream about a certain situation, person, symbol, place, or you might ask for an answer to a specific problem or question. The important thing is to fix the intention of dreaming and remembering the dream when you awaken.

Keep pen and notebook, smartphone or recording device by your bed, ready to take notes if you should wake up suddenly in the night. If upon waking you find the dream has evaporated, lie there for a few moments without thinking about what you have to do in the course of the day. Try to seize on an image from the dream. If nothing else, focus on the feeling the dream gave you.

Promise yourself to write down dreams for at least a week or two. Then, when you have a small group of dream texts to work with, try the following exercise.

Writing Exercise: Working with a Dream

Below follows a four-step method for working with dreams to identify elements that lend themselves to further development.

A practical example is given using the text of a dream recounted to me by a writer, J.B., who has kept detailed dream journals for years, followed by an analysis of some of the elements it contains and some suggestions on how the writer could develop them through dream journaling exercises.

Step One: Write the Dream Down

Give yourself ten minutes to write down the dream as accurately as possible. Here is J.B.'s dream.

> I was in a medieval town, like Florence or Perugia, with towers, balconies, terraces, stairways, tiled rooftops, but there were no roads in between the houses. The only way to get anywhere was to jump or climb, and I was afraid of hurting myself. I felt trapped. As I tried to make my way through the city, some men appeared and told me that I had to go back to elementary school and I was very puzzled. I asked myself: I have two university degrees, why do I have to start over? And I was angry. It seems I was on my way to a conference taking place on the island of Elba and as I approached the conference center, a very modern building made of glass, I looked up at the sky and noticed that the clouds had begun to form curious patterns. As I stood watching, I saw them morph into animal shapes. Domestic animals: sheep, geese, ducks, etc. From white they began to assume pale, pastel colors, light yellow and beige, like decorations in a nursery. The shapes before my eyes became very realistic images of animals and I began to worry that the world was coming to an end.

Suddenly all the animals turned black and morphed into hippopotamuses that descended and dropped into the sea. There were thousands and thousands of furious hippopotamuses that now began to run toward the shore, churning the water and making the earth tremble. I sought refuge inside the glass conference building where, with a group of other people, we tried to find a safe place in the innermost part of the building because we knew the stampede would shatter the glass walls. —J.B.

Step Two: Reflect on the Dream Content

Reread your dream now to see what symbols, patterns, processes, ideas, characters, actions, or feelings stimulate your imagination. Underline or highlight them, reflect on the logic they hold, the connections existing between them, and the messages they may conceal. Put this information in a drawing, chart, deep map, or collage, or simply take notes. Below is a chart based on the dream above, which is very elaborate in terms of setting and references to places. It also contains a logic of unresolved contrasts. Moreover, this dream includes classic psychoanalytical symbols: water, animals, architectural spaces, and pursuit. Take 10–15 minutes for this phase.

- ❖ **Important places:** city, island, sea, nursery, conference center, innermost place
- ❖ **Contrasts:** medieval city—modern conference building
  - domestic animals—hippopotamuses

- sky with domestic animals—sea with hippopotamuses
- pastel colors—black
- no streets/no avenues of communication—conference center

❖ **Parallels in the dream:** elementary school, nursery

❖ **Characters in the dream:** authoritarian figures: *you must start all over*; helpers with whom the dreamer seeks safety

❖ **Emotions in the dream:** fear, entrapment, anger, terror

❖ **Processes:** journey, transformation, destruction, escape, communication

❖ **Actions:** jumping, crawling, being hurt, climbing, transforming, stampeding, hiding

Mythic Elements: Two allusions to myths are immediately apparent: The end of the world and the city as labyrinth. The hippopotamuses charging out of the sea to bring destruction suggest yet another: The Greek myth of the "bull from the sea" sent by Poseidon to King Minos of Crete. In that myth, Pasiphae, wife of King Minos, fell in love with the bull, seduced it, and then gave birth to the Minotaur who was imprisoned in the labyrinth.

Historical Associations: Elba was the island where the despotic Napoleon was exiled for a time.

Step Three: Work with Imagery and Other Elements

In this phase, you will elaborate a few aspects of the dream. Choose any image, set of images, or characters to work with and follow the same procedure outlined earlier in this chapter in the exercise "Working with Spatial Imagery in Dreams." Here the writer might choose the sea, the island of Elba, the streets, the conference center, glass walls, the animals or the allusion to Napoleon.

First, sketch the image and initiate a conversation with it by asking a question. *Who are you? Where do you come from? What do you see?* etc. Write the answer in first person from the image's point of view in a short text of up to 50 words. Then go on to interrogate another element, for example, the contrast of pastel colors and black, and create a three-way dialogue. Give yourself a maximum time limit of thirty minutes for this phase. Take more if you intend to work with more than three images.

As in the previous dream imagery exercise, after the conversation ends, take a break, then return to your desk and write a conclusive sentence in second person. Then go back and reread all that you have written and see what you have learned about the dream.

Step Four: Follow-Up

This phase could take place immediately after concluding the previous ones, or after a period of time, hours, weeks, or even years. Let the meaning of the dream sink in and settle slowly, then use elements from it as writing prompts. There are various ways the writer could develop this particular dream:

- ❖ Write a catastrophic conclusion to the dream or a positive one in a text of 300 words, introducing new characters if desired.

- ❖ Dramatize an encounter with a helper or antagonist in the dream in 300 words.

- ❖ Recast the dream in a modern, realistic setting, transforming the fantastical elements into something more plausible. For example: the hippopotamuses could be clouds, thunder, or bombs, an earthquake. Use the first person and present tense to narrate a story of up to 400 words.

- ❖ Recast the dream into a sci-fi or fantasy mode.

- ❖ Use the dream as a context for a quest narrative. Give the narrator a specific task to solve.

- ❖ Make a collage of words and pictures torn from magazines illustrating something about the dream.

Once you have worked with a sequence of dreams in this way, you will find yourself going back to them to ruminate on their meaning and to seek out images or themes that resonate in your psyche.

Automatic Writing and Free Writing

On October 24th, 1917, a young woman fell into a trance, picked up a pen, and began to write furiously across a white page. Her newlywed husband of four days watched in fascination as her hand scribbled disjointed sentences in an almost illegible scrawl. He found the content of those pages so exciting and profound that he was ready to spend the rest of his life piecing the messages together and trying to understand them. The spirits, however, had other ideas for the young man, the Irish poet, W.B. Yeats. They had come to supply him with new material: "metaphors for poetry."[1] This is the explanation he gives in his introduction to *A Vision*, an intricate philosophical work on symbols, history, myth that the poet claims was dictated by a spirit communicator to his wife through automatic writing. It is doubtful that Mrs. Yeats was putting on a fraud or that she could have invented such a complex system on the spot, so that the genesis of *A Vision* remains one of those mysteries of English literature that will never be solved.

Automatic writing, or writing without conscious intention, gained popularity in the nineteenth century as an after-dinner entertainment, when texts were supposedly dictated telepathically from the spirit world to people in a trance. The writings produced by such methods were nonsensical and fragmentary, and occasionally poetic, comic, or obscene. Sometimes, though, the results were truly astonishing, as Yeats discovered.

In automatic writing, the ego or rational mind concedes its maniacal control. Commenting on the process, Yeats noted how similar the method of spirit communication was to dreaming.[2] The nineteenth century viewed automatic writing as either an authentic manifestation of the spirit world or as a fake, but the contemporary view is that the sources of this phenomenon are internal to the writer, though they may be unknown to him/her or inaccessible through the conscious mind. The French Surrealists André Breton and Paul Éluard performed similar experiments to access unconscious contents.

It's not necessary to fall into a trance in order to experiment with automatic writing. Sit down, seize pen and paper or keyboard and *write.* Results might be surprising, as in this example by a student:

> Black bonnets abound on the white sand. The road turns, turns, turns under the horse's hoof. Umbrellas, umbrellas. Gray stones falling as the waves rush in. The woman rides on, skirts soaked in brine.

The dreamlike imagery and suggested narrative might make an interesting point of departure for a story or poem.

Writing Exercise: Automatic Writing

Decide a time limit of 10–15 minutes and set a timer before you begin. Put yourself in a receptive frame of mind, pick up your pen or start hitting the keys and write as fast as you can, disregarding punctuation, spelling, logic. If you lose the thread of your thought, then leave a blank space, skip down and start again. Don't censor your thoughts as they come. Don't even think about what you're writing and don't reread as you go. When the timer goes off, stop and see what you have written. That's all there is to it.

Some writers suggest focusing attention before beginning to write by asking a question aloud or writing it down, looking at an image, recollecting a feeling or other perception, concentrating on a topic or a person. Others introduce constraints, for example, starting each new thought with the same letter of the alphabet. These suggestions all introduce some form of control into the experience, so that the texts produced are less pure, but they can be revealing all the same.

Since we are working with the soul of place in this book, you could also do this exercise in specific locations, or focus your attention by looking at pictures of places, or perhaps, handling your talismans of place.

Some people will click with this type of exercise immediately, others may never do so. A few sessions will deepen the experience. If you let yourself go with the flow for a while, automatic writing may teach you something about the way you use language and the way sounds and images cohere in your imagination.

Free Writing

Throughout this book, when you have been invited to write for ten minutes or produce 300 words on a topic, you have been working with the technique of "free writing," a more controlled process than automatic writing that shares the same aim of tapping into our unconscious stream of energy and ideas. This fundamental concept in creative writing was pioneered by Dorothea Brande in her groundbreaking work, *Becoming a Writer*, first published in 1934 and rediscovered by novelist and writing teacher John Gardner in 1980. In free writing, emphasis is given to fluidity and freedom from censorship, fear, expectations, or constraints of any kind, including grammar, spelling, logic, or social conventions. The goal is not to create a polished text, but to explore your own resources and learn how to access them. Free writing is a pre-writing and preparatory phase for generating material and seeking out new directions.

Brande suggests that to give best results, free writing should be practiced within a regular schedule, ideally first thing in the morning, maintained with rigorous discipline, letting nothing come between the writer and the intention to write. The actual content of what you write is unimportant, at least at first. What matters is to link the physical act of writing with the unconscious flow of ideas. To use Brande's words: to hitch the unconscious to your writing arm.[3] Over time, she argued, this disciplined approach will allow the writer to gain entry to a deeply buried treasure trove of writing material.

In more recent times, Brande's methods have been developed by celebrated writing teachers such as Natalie Goldberg and Peter Elbow and have been extended into other domains as well. Julia Cameron, author of the internationally renowned guide to reawakening blocked creativity, *The Artist's Way*, bases her extraordinary and highly successful system on free writing, or "morning pages," as the key to unleashing our creative energies in any field of endeavor.

Writing Exercise: Create a Free Writing Routine on Soul of Place

Many of the writing prompts in this book, especially those calling for short texts of 50–300 words, or ten minutes, are free writing exercises. If you have never tried Brande's experiment of adhering to a regular morning schedule, and you'd like to attempt it with exercises on soul of place, here are some suggestions.

First, decide on a long-term schedule with a minimum of six weeks. Then set aside some time every morning to dedicate to writing practice. If an hour seems too long because of your daily commitments, try to allot thirty minutes and stick to it regularly, come hell or high water.

Creating a structure for the entire period will give you focus. Pick a broad theme for each week. For example: Week One: Interiors; Week Two: Landscapes and Nature, Maps; Week Three: A specific site from your childhood; Week Four: Food; Week Five: Dreams and Automatic Writing; Week Six: No limits, no constraints. Or go by categories: Week One: Islands; Week Two: Grandma's House; Week Three: Trout Fishing; Week Four: Dogs; Week Five: Trains. Write down the weekly topics on a calendar and keep it handy on your desk for reference.

Stick to your schedule. When you sit down to write, choose any prompt from this book and apply it to your topic. Give yourself the goal of producing 200 words or two pages per sitting. Keep at it for at least six weeks and at the end judge your results for yourself.

Suggested Reading

Dorothea Brande, *Becoming a Writer*
Julia Cameron, *The Artist's Way*
Naomi Epel, *Writers Dreaming*
Natalie Goldberg, *Writing Down the Bones*
Susan M. Tiberghien, *One Year to a Writing Life*
W.B. Yeats, *A Vision*

⌒

Another Technique for Tapping the Unconscious: The Theory of Correspondences or Signatures

The English writer Mary Butts (1890–1937), like many writers of her generation, was intrigued by symbolism, occultism, and myth and their connection to the budding science of psychology. One theory that particularly interested her was the theory of correspondences, also known as the doctrine of signatures, developed by Emanuel Swedenborg (1688–1772), and elaborated from the ideas of the Neo-Platonists. This theory suggests that the divine, spiritual, and human spheres, while situated on different planes, mirror each other and are linked by a tightly knit and all pervasive mesh of symbolic connections or analogies called *correspondences* or *signatures*. For example: the physical light perceived by our eye corresponds on the spiritual plane to human wisdom, which in turn corresponds to its divine manifestation: God's wisdom, etc. All natural phenomena are signatures for entities and qualities existing at a higher level. Swedenborg's theories influenced many writers, such as Johann Wolfgang Goethe, William Blake, W.B. Yeats, Ralph Waldo Emerson, and C.G. Jung. For Mary Butts, every mood and perception of our interior life has a counterpart or correspondence in the natural world.

> Man passes there amid a forest of symbols...
>
> —*Charles Baudelaire*

The journal of Mary Butts reveals that she studied her life, emotions, and environment in search of these correspondences—encrypted information that could unveil the contents of her own unconscious mind, reveal hidden aspects of persons, situations, events, and even predict the future. To be aware of the link or correspondence between an ordinary gesture and a higher level was to enter a state of heightened consciousness. In her journal, Butts captures a few such moments. For example, while she is standing at a sink, washing dirt off potatoes, this humble contact with the elements of earth and water triggers an epiphany. In another instance, she clutches a worn coin in her hand and tries to feel the negative charge it may hold, connected to some negative event.

The theory of correspondences or signatures suggests that our environment is densely packed with messages pertaining to the future, past, and present, which we may learn to interpret for different ends. In my novel, *Signatures in Stone*, I have developed and applied this theory as follows:

> We are constantly immersed in a network of signs and symbols whose meaning eludes us, but which, if only we could read them, would reveal every detail of our past and even predict our future. Like anticipatory echoes, they tingle in our consciousness, building in crescendo until the event they herald becomes fully manifest. Afterwards, they linger for a time before being drowned out by a new tide of signs rushing in upon us. Such signatures are everywhere—a glove dropped in the street, an unusual design of seaweed

washed up on the beach, a picture postcard addressed to a stranger, slipped in between the pages of a borrowed book.

Signatures often take the form of curious coincidences, but we usually fail to notice when they present themselves. For example, on your way downstairs one morning, you nearly stumble on a toy boat left on the stairs by a neighbor's child. At breakfast an article on the front page of *The Times* catches your eye, telling of some catastrophe at sea. Stepping out to the street, you nearly collide with a delivery boy carrying a bucket of live eels to a nearby restaurant. As the day passes, you overhear snatches of conversation in which the words "water" or "island" are repeated. Returning home, you find the pipes have burst and a puddle has formed on the bathroom floor.

Now, the ordinarily inattentive mind will not pause to consider these coincidences. Many people would not even notice that they are connected one to another, as it were, thematically to the concept of "sea voyage." But suppose the very next day, urgent business affairs oblige you to book passage to New York. These insignificant events occurring throughout the previous day may then be understood as a premonitory experience composed of dozens of minor "correspondences" or "signatures." Most likely, you will remember but a few fragments of the mosaic. But if you could piece them all together and properly interpret them, you'd not only foresee your journey, but also the outcome of the business affairs taking you abroad. We are never attentive enough to what is happening around us.[4]

Writing Exercise: Find the Correspondences in Your Environment

Scour your immediate environment for signatures or correspondences. Start with the random arrangement of books on your desk, the leavings on the table when a meal is concluded. Take a drawer, dump out the contents, and see what you *see*. What "secrets" of the past does the random arrangement of items reveal—what future event could it be predicting? Take your random array of objects and use this as a basis for a free write or lyric essay.

Suggested Reading

Mary Butts, *The Journal of Mary Butts*
Linda Lappin, *Signatures in Stone*

Symbolic Geometry

Another way to tap into the unconscious is to work with archetypal spatial forms: the pyramid, circle, spiral, mandala, square, cube, dome, arch that sometimes occur in our dreams. You might use these forms as conceptual models to link ideas, events, places, or characters of a story or poem together in triangles, squares, circles. In writing my first novel, *The Etruscan*, I connected characters through triangles. Or you may use these shapes as structural forms to organize the development of a story, poem, or essay. In visual or concrete poetry, the typographical arrangement of words on the page is as important to conveying the message of the poem as the words themselves or as the other poetic devices used, such as rhyme, imagery, etc.

Writing Exercise: Symbolic Forms

Choose an exercise from this book that appeals to you and write a poem, prose poem, or fragment up to 30 words. Write your text in the form of a circle, square, triangle, spiral, labyrinth, to see how the spatial arrangement of words on the page influences your imagination. Experiment with different forms to see the different effect.

Writing Exercise: Visualize a Text

Take a short poetic text or fragment you have written about a place of 10–25 words and see if it suggests any geometrical or other spatial or visual forms to you. Collect some materials for drawing or collage, large sheets of paper, colored pens, magazines or newspapers. Draw or paint a background, or tear pictures from a magazine to provide a context or illustration for a collage. Insert your text either writing by hand, or using letters cut out from a newspaper.

Labyrinths: A Mythic Space

For eons, the labyrinth or maze has appeared in myth, literature, visual and performing arts as a theme, setting, and a metaphor symbolizing the uncertainties, intricacies, and entanglements of our life journey; bewilderment and entrapment; the convolutions of destiny and of the mind. As an icon and physical structure, it appears in the sacred art and architecture of many great civilizations of the past: Minoan, Egyptian, Greek, Roman, Etruscan, Hindu, Native American. As a decorative or symbolic pattern, it has been painted on pottery, carved on cave walls, paved on gothic cathedral floors, and tattooed in the body-art designs of primitive cultures. It is a frequent motif in ancient and medieval art and architecture, and later, in renaissance, baroque and modern garden design. In many religious traditions through-out the ages it has represented the hero's/heroine's journey to the center, where the secret of iden-tity, immortality, or initiation is concealed. As a symbol of whole-ness and completion, it is con-nected to the spiral and like the spiral it evokes the greater cycles around us and their role in the processes of regeneration. It is one of the dominant metaphors in modern and contemporary literature and philosophy.

> I got immeshed in a network of turns unknown. I was lost.
>
> —*Charlotte Brontë*

Literary Labyrinths

The most celebrated labyrinth in literature was that of Crete, which, the Greek myth tells us, was built by King Minos's architect, Daedalus, to house the Cretan king's monstrous step-son, the Minotaur, half bull and half man, who demanded a sacrifice of Athenian youth every nine years. The hero Theseus set off from Athens to put an end to this horror, taking the place of one of the young men chosen for sacrifice. When he reached Crete, Minos's daughter, Ariadne, fell in love with him, and taught him how to navigate the labyrinth by fastening one end of a ball of twine or "clew" to the entrance. Theseus slayed the Minotaur and escaped with the young Athenians, along with Ariadne, to the island of Naxos, where they performed a special dance to celebrate their liberation and where poor Ariadne was left behind.

Throughout the history of archaeology, many attempts have been made to identify the ruins of Minos's labyrinth, for which different locations have been suggested: the ruins of the palace of Knossos, natural caves at Skotino, and a tunnel system in Gortyn, all on Crete. Some evidence points to the fact that the labyrinth may originally have been a dance floor where some form of ritual enactment of the above myth was performed, connected to a "Lady of the Labyrinth," a form of *genius loci*, and the concept of rebirth. In ancient Greece the term labyrinth was also used metaphorically, as we do today, to indicate an argument that will lead us back to its beginning, if we aren't devoured at midpoint by the monster within.

From Dante's *Inferno* with its descending spirals, to our own era, the labyrinth has been a primary metaphor for the way we experience the unfolding of our lives and acquire knowledge of ourselves and the world. It has had a special appeal to postmodernists. Franz Kafka, Jorge Luis Borges, Alain Robbe-Grillet, Lawrence Durrell, Italo Calvino, Umberto Eco, John Fowles, Francesca Duranti, and Orhan Pamuk, are just a few twentieth-century and contemporary writers who have all employed the labyrinth as a structural or symbolic device in their work to express paradox, the caprices of destiny, or liminal experience. In Calvino's *Invisible Cities*, it is a symbol for the contemporary city; for Umberto Eco, it is a symbol for knowledge and narrative; for Borges, it symbolizes writing itself, which shapes us as we shape it. For John Fowles and Lawrence Durrell, it is a supreme symbol for the novel. The maze or labyrinth remains a popular theme in mainstream fiction and fantasy, as in Kate Mosse's historical-mythic-suspense novel, *Labyrinth* and Guillermo del Toro's dark fantasy film, *Pan's Labyrinth*.

If you have ever wanted to play with this myth, here's your chance.

◦───

Labyrinth Writing Exercises:

As theme, setting, metaphor, and structural device, the labyrinth offers interesting possibilities as a writing prompt. The labyrinth configures stories, and in a way it is a story within a story. What happens to the character before entering and after exiting a labyrinth are completely different stories from what takes place within it. In myth, to enter and exit a labyrinth is to be reborn. Before trying one of the exercises below, take some time to familiarize yourself with different forms and images of the labyrinth. Writing teacher Susan B. Tiberghien suggests tracing its pattern with your finger to better absorb its meaning on a physical plane. Start by free writing 50 words on the subject of "labyrinth." Then go on to do the following:

The Labyrinth as Personal Situation

Apply the image of the labyrinth to a personal problem you have solved. How did you sort out the pathways and make your way to the core? Who or what was the Minotaur in the center of the labyrinth? What conflict did you need to overcome? Who provided the thread that guided you out again? Write up to 500 words.

The Labyrinth as Physical Space

The back alleys of Venice, Rome, Florence, the Left Bank of Paris, North African souks, Greek and Turkish fishing villages, dense forests, natural caves, and rocky canyons have repeatedly been described as "labyrinths," as have the bewildering corridors of cruise ships, hospitals, prisons, and hotels. Remember those hallways in Stephen King's *The Shining?*

Does the symbol "labyrinth" fit any places you have visited or explored? Narrate an experience of getting lost or finding your way through such a labyrinth in 300 words.

Fiction writers: create an artificial labyrinth or labyrinthine structure as the setting of a story. Consider that the labyrinth is often paired with the act of detection. The story of Theseus in the labyrinth may be one of the world's earliest detective stories.

The Labyrinth as a Structural Device in Fiction

There are two main labyrinth patterns: the unicursal and the multicursal. In a unicursal pattern, there is a single, continuous line looped and coiled around a center, to which it eventually leads. In a multicursal pattern, we have an intricate interweaving of separate lines or pathways, branching off in many directions, some leading to dead ends. A multicursal labyrinth may have more than one exit and entrance, and no center at all.

The symbolic values of the two figures are quite different from each other. The unicursal labyrinth will guide us to our destination if we abandon ourselves to its random detours, but the multicursal labyrinth makes us lose our way, compels us to stop and make decisions about where to go, which may or may not be lethal. The unicursal charts a quest for the sacred guided by faith; the multicursal leads us along through trial and error. In both cases, we cannot see or understand the pattern until we are out of it.

The labyrinth can also be an intriguing structural device for plot design. In a unicursal plot, we would have a basic story line evolving towards a conclusion despite a series of deviations and detours. We often find this in fairy tales, for example, when the hero, pursued by the villain, shape shifts into different forms to escape being caught, becoming a hare, a fish, a candle flame, while the villain changes his shape accordingly. In a multicursal plot, however, we would have different plotlines looped around each other and occasionally petering out into dead ends or branching out into other possibilities. Postmodernists have been particularly attracted to the idea of the multicursal narrative composed of bifurcating timelines that would allow seemingly incompatible events to occur simultaneously, such as a character's death and his rescue from death. One famous example is Borges' enigmatic "The Garden of Forking Paths." Novelist John Fowles reached for a similar effect when he wrote multiple endings for *The French Lieutenant's Woman*.

Another example of a multicursal plot design is Alice Munro's short story, "Carried Away. " In this story, we find several intersecting plotlines: Louisa's aborted epistolary love affair with Jack, whose face she will never see, although he frequents the library where she works; her marriage, through which she acquires a social status and a "normal life"; Jack's own marriage and the dreadful accident through which he is decapitated; and lastly, the final hallucination in which Louisa meets Jack again, who is not dead, physically resembles someone else and reveals his love for her. The story then ends with a strange flashback to her first day in town, evoking events that preceded the opening pages of the story. In this circular structure, the center of the labyrinth is Jack, or Louisa's love for this man who perpetually eluded her. The story works through a labyrinth toward its beginning.

Writing Exercise: A Multicursal Plot

Write a short narrative with a unicursal plot: one main line of events evolving toward a conclusion despite a series of deviations and detours. Then try to rewrite it with a multicursal plot pattern, developing the deviations, detours, bifurcations, and sidelines into new stories, the outcomes of which may contradict each other. You might even draw a labyrinth to help you map the development of the narrative branches. There is no word count for this.

Walking the Labyrinth

The ancient Roman custom of using labyrinths in mosaic floor design was later appropriated by Christianity in decorating the floors of the great gothic cathedrals in France and elsewhere. One example is found in Chartres cathedral, the most often reproduced unicursal labyrinth in the world. The labyrinth traced on the floor between the portal and the altar charts the journey that the seeker must undergo on his or her spiritual evolution towards the center symbolizing God.

Labyrinths in churches were used at special times as an aid to prayer through movement. In medieval times, "walking the labyrinth" on the floor of a sacred place was believed to substitute the actual experience of pilgrimage if a person was too ill or infirm to undertake a journey to the Holy Land. In recent years, there has been a rebirth of interest in this symbol and of its application in the Christian church. Many churches now re-enact labyrinth rituals as part of their worship services in the period of Lent. On Fridays from Lent to All Souls Day, the labyrinth of Chartres may sometimes be walked. Labyrinths for meditation in movement have also been adopted by Jewish circles as well as by other traditions.

High on the hillside above a Cretan village I know, some-one has built a rudimentary labyrinth, a beaten trail through the dust and scrub, lined with rocks, modeled on the pattern of the Chartres labyrinth. Whenever I return to that village, I like to perform this labyrinth exercise divided into four phases. If you are lucky enough to find a labyrinth like the ones in Chartres or San Francisco's Grace Cathedral, use this or invent your own ritual. Or try drawing a labyrinth with chalk on the floor, if you can find a large enough area, or on a driveway or quiet street. P.L. Travers, the author of the *Mary Poppins* series, once suggested that the best way to walk a labyrinth was barefoot.

❖ **Phase 1. Turn Inward:** As you begin your journey toward the center, find your own center, empty your mind, let go of the details of everyday life, focus on your problem, need, desire, request, or lack. Let your body feel the rhythm of the turns.

❖ **Phase 2. Stand Still in the Core:** When you reach the heart of the labyrinth, meditate, pray, or simply open yourself to feelings, influences, ideas, images, or insight that may come.

❖ **Phase 3. Return Outward:** As you leave the labyrinth, be aware of your connection to the world surrounding you and to the spirit or higher energy, whatever name you give to it, always at work in the world. Bring the awareness of your connection with that force back into the world.

❖ **Phase 4. Write about the experience.**

Suggested Reading

Jorge Luis Borges, *Labyrinths*
Italo Calvino, *Invisible Cities*
Francesca Duranti, *Personal Effects*
Lawrence Durrell, *The Dark Labyrinth*
Umberto Eco, *The Name of the Rose*
Alice Munro, "Carried Away"
P.L. Travers, *What the Bee Knows*

Animals and Totems

In the previous section, we met with a mythical animal, the Minotaur symbolizing the forces of the unconscious. Animals are among the most frequent symbols populating our myths, fairytales, and dreams. We see these embodiments of the life force as akin to us, as mirrors of our instinctual selves, and yet completely *other.* At home in their environment in a way that we can never be (but perhaps once were), they remind us of what we have lost. We admire the powers that set them apart from us: their miraculous ability to fly, see in the dark, breathe underwater, or to renew themselves by shedding their skins or regenerating a tail. Their strength, speed, voracity, beauty, or cunning all lend specific animals their peculiar magic of metaphor with which we at times identify ourselves. It was those very qualities the shaman acquired when he put on the mask of his totem in order to perform a healing ritual or seek guidance for his community in times of crisis.

In traditional societies, the totem-animal had a deep psychic connection to both individuals and clans as guide, guardian, and ancestor. To study the totem was to know oneself and to discover one's strengths and weaknesses, necessary to the art of survival. Even nowadays we often have our totems, though we may not recognize them as such, and sometimes indulge ourselves by considering ourselves or others as "dog people," "sex kittens," "studs," "lions," "beasts," and "bunnies," while criticizing others as "snakes," "rats," "sheep," or "cold fish." Animals help us know who we are and who we would like to be.

Animals are also manifestations of the soul of place. Cats prowling the ruins of Rome, camels in the desert, solitary donkeys on sun-baked Grecian hills, these may be hackneyed subjects for picture postcards or souvenir calendars because they are so "typical"—yet undeniably they are authentic expressions of some aspects of soul of place given their ties to the environment or their function in the overall ecology and economy of a place. For critic Walter Benjamin, the *genius loci* of his own Paris neighborhood was embodied in his concierge's cat.

We all have our private menageries reflecting our personal experience of the animal kingdom, including the relationships we may have had with pets, our encounters with domestic or wild animals in their native or artificial habitats, and our own affinities with certain animals. Pick some to write about and try the exercises below.

Writing Exercise: Neighboring Lives

Poet Jeffrey Greene became so curious about the boars living in the wild around his village in Burgundy, that he would rise in the night, throw a coat over his pajamas and go out searching for them, observing them for hours from a thicket. This passion led him to research the natural history, mythology, and gastronomy of boars, and to write a book about his experience, part memoir, part nature writing, *The Golden Bristled Boar.* Is there an animal *you* feel a special affinity for? Or one that shares your space, hidden in a hedge at the bottom of your garden? Write a short text of 200 words.

Writing Exercise: Close Encounters

Have you ever had "too close" an encounter with:

❖ a poisonous animal

❖ a ferocious mammal

❖ an exotic bird or winged creature

❖ an animal that had strayed from its habitat into your own living space

❖ a reptile

❖ a mouse

Free write for ten minutes on one of the above.

Write a narrative episode in third person and present tense, emphasizing the conflict in 300 words.

Writing Exercise: See Life Through Other Eyes

Franz Kafka's Gregory Samsa, a humble clerk, woke up one morning and found he had been turned into a cockroach. Through magic learned from his Yaqui *brujo*, Carlos Castaneda became a crow. Virginia Woolf described the life of Elizabeth Barrett Browning through the eyes of her cocker spaniel, Flush. Paul Bowles's hallucinatory story *Allal* about the exchange of consciousness between a Moroccan boy and a snake (and the dire consequences of that exchange) is a tour de force recreating alien and alienating perceptions.

Free write for ten minutes about a moment in your daily life seen through the eyes of an animal. Many people are tempted to use their pets for this exercise, but reach for something more exotic.

Fiction writers: write a short scene involving a conflict between a person and an animal, using the animal's point of view.

Writing Exercise: Bugs and Creepy Crawlies

Wherever we live, we are immersed in a mesh of tiny lives, often undetected, with which we share our environment. Insects have their own mystique. Although moths, butterflies, fireflies, or crickets bring us delight, insects are widely reviled in Western culture as negative, infernal, and bringers of disease. All insects have a deep connection to the psyche and have something to teach us, embodying powerful life forces of reproduction, hunger, and survival.

Write about an insect connected to a place where you lived in 300 words.

Choose five insects or arachnids and write five short texts of 50 words. Illustrate with your own drawings.

Fiction writers: Write about an insect as metaphor in 300 words.

⌒

Katabasis, the Journey Downwards: Using Myths for Inspiration

Once upon a time, we made sense of ourselves and our world by telling a story, conjuring an archetype, or creating a symbol. The myths, symbols, and stories that sprang from our imagination in those distant days are some of the most powerful and enduring creations of world culture. The old myths still move us, reverberating in our unconscious, in our dreams, and in the stories we keep telling and retelling. From our earliest bards to popular authors J.K. Rowling and Dan Brown, writers have looked to mythology for inspiration, plot patterns, character prototypes, and imagery. Previously in this chapter, we looked at an example of an ancient myth connected with a place, the Cretan labyrinth, that offers insights and suggestions for your writing practice. In this section we'll look at another myth dealing with a spiritually charged environment: the underworld.

The journey to the underworld, in Greek called *"katabasis,"* is a recurring trope in mythology, religion, fairy tales, literature, fantasy, and films, as varied as *Black Orpheus* or *Lord of the Rings*.

Joseph Campbell, the world authority on myth, claimed that *katabasis* represents a specific phase in an overarching myth of the hero or heroine manifest in every culture on the globe, to which he gave the name of the "monomyth." In his seminal work, *The Hero with a Thousand Faces*, he sums up the monomyth: A hero sets out from home and travels to a supernatural realm where he encounters powerful forces and engages in a decisive test.[5] He then returns home with the power to bestow boons on his community. Campbell identified three main phases in the hero's journey: the call to adventure, the road of trials, the goal or boon. These three phases may also be described as separation/departure, initiation, and return, and can be traced in most stories dealing with katabasis.

According to Campbell, *katabasis* begins with a "call to initiation" and separation from family and home environment. The hero or heroine is compelled by some great need to seek out someone or something that can only be found in the underworld, or to return something that belongs there. In the Greek myth, Orpheus goes on his journey to bring back his dead wife. In Vergil's *Aeneid*, Aeneas goes in search of his father to find out the future of Rome. In *Lord of the Rings*, Frodo climbs alone into Mt. Doom to throw the ring into a chasm. Whether traveling into the deeps of the earth or into the depths of oneself, *katabasis* is an experience of solitude, mourning, danger, and often estrangement from what we hold most dear: our sense of who we are. Luckily, a helper usually appears before departure to prepare the hero for adventure, provide a map or magic object to help navigate the territory, or offer services as a guide.

In Greek mythology, the underworld was the realm of the dead, having its own very realistic geography and landscape, with whirlpools, deserts, giant boulders, massive trees, fiery lakes, marshes and mud—often described by ancient poets in very concrete detail. In other traditions, it isn't always "under the ground"—it may be beneath or across the sea, in a desert or forest, enclosed in a mountain such as the Chinese hell, Feng-Du, which the Chinese imagined to be a series of efficiently run prisons. The underworld is usually accessed by an actual cave or tunnel situated in a real place or by a magic entry existing within something quite ordinary. In C.S. Lewis's *The Lion, the Witch, and the Wardrobe*, that door to the other world was behind old clothes hanging in a closet. In *Black Orpheus*, Marcel Camus's retelling of the Greek myth, it is found in the basement beneath the Bureau of Missing Persons in modern-day Brazil. As Rene Daumal suggests in his allegorical novel *Mount Analogue*, the door to the invisible must be visible for the adventure to take place.

In this shadowy, alien realm, the protagonist undergoes tests and trials and may be captured, imprisoned or enslaved. Often, like Orpheus or his Japanese counterpart, Izanagi, he will meet dead loved ones whom he is powerless to rescue or who have important messages to deliver. During the journey, the hero or heroine will encounter allies and enemies, lose a possession or receive a gift, find a treasure, discover his or her true origins, acquire knowledge, and/or achieve liberation for him or herself or for another before returning to the light of day. It is easy to see how this formula underpins many fictional narratives. It also appears disguised in many memoirs in which quest, conflict, resolution, and transformation are key phases.

At the peak of the action, conflict occurs with an antagonist, who may be the reigning entity, like the Minotaur or Pluto.

But it can also be a person, an animal, a form of addiction, a self-destructive tendency, a fear, disease, an unpleasant side of ourselves, an evil twin. This confrontation marks the moment of initiation. If that initiation is successful, the hero or heroine will receive a new identity, power, or knowledge to take back to the world above. If he fails, he will not escape alive.

Psychologists tell us that *katabasis* is an exploration of the individual or collective unconscious where we may uncover repressed and buried instincts, desires, emotions, secrets, and unacknowledged needs. This is the realm of chaos and the irrational, and yet a source of creative and vital power. It is home to what depth psychologist C.G. Jung called the shadow—the dark side of our nature that we cannot easily recognize because it contains repressed, negative, and unfavorable aspects of ourselves that Jungian psychologists believe must be integrated into our personality to achieve full realization of our true self.

Writing Exercise:
Free Writes on Hell and the Underworld

The following free writes can be adapted to many moods. You could write about hell as a personal experience with negative forces, imagine a fantasy world, or take a humorous or ironic approach.

Find a place in your home or neighborhood that could be the entryway into the underworld. Write 100 words describing the place.

Think of a real landscape that you have seen in pictures or actually visited that might make a suitable setting for the underworld. Describe it in 100 words

Imagine an antagonist in your personal hell. Write a short description of 50 words.

You are about to make a journey to the underworld. What will you take with you and why? Write 200 words

You have returned from hell. What did you do there? What did you bring back? Write 200 words.

Writing Exercise: Complete Katabasis

If you are intrigued by this myth, below is an exercise that will lead you through all the phases of *katabasis*. Using elements in your immediate environment, write a narrative of descent based on the patterns just discussed. As in the free writes above, it can be applied to a personal experience, be serious, humorous, or take the form of a fantasy.

Create a character and the circumstances through which he or she finds himself alone, separated from family or community. Give him or her a goal to reach, a quest to fulfill, a problem to solve.

I. Imagine the portal to your underworld. Situate it within something *ordinary*. In E.M. Forster's short story "The Celestial Omnibus," the hero finds himself transported to literary heaven by a bus that leaves each day from the square at dawn.

2. The portal may be guarded by someone or something so that it is not *immediately* visible or perhaps not easily accessible. Identify and describe the guardian and give your seeker a means with which to deal with him or her or it.

3. Narrate the journey farther down (or across or through), describing the passage across the threshold of the

underworld. What sense perceptions or landmarks signal entry into the other realm? What concrete details might convey the seeker's emotions?

4. Describe the landscape of the underworld.

5. Create an encounter with a helper or guide in any form.

6. Meet the shadow. Describe its physical appearance. What makes it so fearsome?

7. Narrate the conflict, and find a resolution. What gift or boon is given or withheld?

8. Bring your character back into the light of day. Focus on the moment when she exits the underworld. What does the seeker find at the moment of transition back into daily reality? How does the world look through transformed eyes?

Suggested Reading

Dante Alighieri, *The Inferno*
Joseph Campbell, *The Hero with a Thousand Faces*
Ovid, *Metamorphoses*

⁓

Bringing It All Together: Final Projects

1. Write a postcard narrative from the underworld. Or one from Theseus or the Minotaur.

2. Describe a neighborhood or house from your past as a labyrinth.

3. The best way to know a place is to dream it. Apply this to a place in your life in an essay of 500 words.

4. Make a deep map of a fantasy world.

5. Write a quest narrative or lyric essay dealing with a real labyrinth.

6. Decide what animal best expresses the soul of place of your neighborhood. Write 200 words on this topic. Or write about your totem animal.

7. Use synesthesia as a prompt for automatic writing.

8. Use animals or insects and food as a prompt for automatic writing. Or write about feeding an animal.

9. Write a quest narrative involving an animal or insect.

10. Go back to the list of neighborhood places given at the end of Chapter Two. Use these locations as inspirations for free writing or automatic writing experiments.

11. Keep a dream diary for at least a month, then use recurring place or space imagery in a lyric essay, fictional narrative, or poem.

12. Write about a phobia connected to an animal or a food in a personal essay or short fiction passage.

13. Practice automatic writing in different locations in your house.

14. Find some correspondences or signatures in the room where you are sitting now. Write about them in 150 words.

15. Think of a writer or character in literature you admire. Write a passage of fiction involving a dream the person had.

16. Write about a place in your house that is highly symbolic for you.

17. Write a fictional dream involving loss or recovery.

18. Write a lyric essay or quest narrative in a unicursal or multicursal pattern.

19. Describe food or hunger in the underworld.

20. Write about a waking dream you once experienced, when you weren't sure if you were asleep or not.

21. Write about a food you dreamed, or one that doesn't exist, in 300 words.

22. Look into the bottom of your coffee mug or beer glass and imagine there's a face or scene. Write about it in 300 words.

23. Every house is the embodiment of the inner life of its inhabitants. What does your house say about you?

---

[1] W.B. Yeats, *A Vision*, New York: Collier Books, 1966. p. 8.

[2] Ibid., p. 22.

[3] Dorothea Brande, *Becoming a Writer*, Los Angeles: Tarcher, 1934, p. 69.

[4] Linda Lappin, *Signatures in Stone*, New York: Pleasure Boat Studio, 2013, p. 41.

[5] Joseph Campbell, *The Hero with a Thousand Faces*, Princeton: Bollingen Books. 1949, p. 24.

A Final Thought About
Your Writing Space

Some authors adhere superstitiously to rituals when it comes to their writing practice: using a special pen, wearing certain clothes, writing at a certain time of day, or working at a special desk or in a certain room. Virginia Woolf once claimed that a woman can't write fiction without a room of her own, and most writers would agree that a space where you can be alone is an absolute necessity. Your writing studio can be a humble one, Stephen King suggests; you just need to be able to shut the door. Fiction writer Raymond Carver used to reminisce about writing in his car when he needed a break from a bustling household routine.

What I would like you to consider now is the way in which your present writing environment interacts with your imagination. Look around your writing room—filled with electronic or mechanical equipment, supplies, furniture, books, and perhaps mementos, artwork, talismans, or other objects imbued with personal significance and stamped with your life stories. Whether it is cozy, Zen, artsy, or high-tech, do you feel comfortable when you sit down to write and ready to turn inwards? What about the colors, materials, lighting? Do they contribute to an atmosphere conducive to your creativity? Is your desk burdened with clutter from old projects gathering dust? Does the overall space correspond to an image or ideal that you have outgrown?

If you discover that you aren't satisfied with your writing space, is there something simple you could do to change or rearrange it? I am not suggesting repainting or calling in an interior decorator to create a "writerly" environment, but rather reinvestigating your space to see if it corresponds to your current needs, desires, or fantasies. Through this book, you have perhaps discovered ways in which our surroundings reflect inner worlds, and at the same time mold them. Apply this concept to the room where you work. Try some of the following exercises and then see if there is something you'd like to change in your writing room.

1. Write a third person narrative about yourself working at your desk in 300 words.

2. Let your writing desk or table speak to you in second person in a free write of 300 words.

3. Write about a writing project you abandoned in 300 words.

4. Free write about a photograph or artwork in your writing room.

5. Write about a symbolic object or talisman in your writing room.

6. Write about an ideal writing space in 300 words.

7. Describe the soul of place of your writing room.

Afterword

The landscape of Greece is so saturated in myths, superstitions, and history, that you can hardly make your way across it without being ensnared, or so Patrick Leigh Fermor once suggested. I believe the same could be said for nearly every environment. The places we live are densely inscribed with stories, symbols, and lives, waiting to be untangled and read.

This book has been constructed from the outside inwards, from landscapes to interiors and house furnishings, the food on our kitchen table, and lastly inner spaces of dreams, myths, and fantasies. There are an infinite number of ways these exercises may be combined, reworked, or reshuffled to yield unexpected results. Few are intended to be "recipes" for polished pieces. Most are meant as experiments for generating new material.

The soul of place is like an invisible net cast up at times from within a house, neighborhood, or landscape to draw us into its labyrinthine folds. We never know what we will find there once we start wandering around: the taste of warm strawberries plucked from the ground on a lazy June afternoon, the smell of grandma's hairnet kept in the top dresser drawer, or something older, not pertaining to us personally, a fragment of a myth, the marble profile of a god, bloodstained relics from a battle that may have ended centuries ago but still seems to be going on.

All writers have their psycho-geographies—our maps of terrains trekked across or still to conquer, with their islands, oceans, highways, and parking lots, cemeteries, signposts, landing strips or ley lines. I hope that through these exercises you have had the opportunity to revisit a few places of your own to uncover some meanings and mysteries there.

Acknowledgments

I would like to thank a few writing teachers who have contributed to the experiences gathered here. First, Donald Justice, who when I moved abroad, urged me to "Keep a journal of your experiences. Not your emotions. Just things and events." It was wise advice. I would also like to thank more recent teachers, Thomas E. Kennedy, whose help has been invaluable; Susan M. Tiberghien, author *One Year to a Writing Life*, whose insightful workshops at the Geneva Writers Conference resonated with some of my own deepest interests; A.E. Stallings, whose Muses' Workshop at the Athens Poetry Centre gave me much food for thought; and Evan Rail, who taught me how much fun it is to write about food.

Special thanks also to the students of the University Study Abroad Consortium (USAC) literary travel writing/memoir course at the University of the Tuscia, in Viterbo, Italy, who served as my guinea pigs, along with those of the Centro Pokkoli writing workshops and retreats, who allowed me to test and develop the material included here. I would particularly like to thank Francesca Toso, an early Pokkoli participant, who gave me the idea of writing this book. I express grateful thanks to USAC for the career development grant I received enabling me to attend the Athens Poetry Workshop in 2011 and to the European Association of Creative Writing Programs for the opportunity to present my research on deep maps and myth at two of their annual conferences.

And last but not least, I would like to thank my husband Sergio for his tireless support, without which I couldn't have carried on.

~

Credits and Permissions

From D.H. Lawrence, Extracts from *Sea and Sardinia* by D.H. Lawrence reprinted by permission of Pollinger Limited (www. pollingerltd.com) on behalf of the Estate of Frieda Lawrence Ravagli.

From "A Lost Tradition," in *The Rough Field,* by John Montague, copyright © 1972 by John Montague, Wake Forest University Press. Used by permission of Wake University Press. By permission of The Gallery Press, Ireland, Loughcrew, Ireland. By permission, The Exile Writers, Ontario, Canada.

From *Du Côté de chez Swann,* by Marcel Proust, Gallimard, translation by Linda Lappin.

The author would also like to thank *The Writer Magazine* for permission granted to use material originally published in the publication and later revised for inclusion in this book: "See With Fresh Eyes," November 2009. "Katabasis, Your Journey to Hell and Back," September 2013, "Pilgrims and Seekers," March 2014. "On the Street: The Art of Flanerie," August 2014. The magazine is on the web at writermag.com

Bibliography

Anson, Bernard. *Carmen Via.* Rome-The Hague: Semar Publishing, 2006.

Augé, Marc. *Non-Places.* New York: Verso, 2009.

Bach, Lisa (ed.). *Her Fork in the Road: Women Celebrate Food and Travel.* Palto Alto: Travelers' Tales, 2005.

Bachelard, Gaston. *The Poetics of Space.* Boston: Beacon Press, 1994.

Benjamin, Walter. *The Arcades Project.* New York: Belknap Press, 2002.

Bergson, Henri. *Key Writings.* New York: Continuum International Publishing, 2002.

Bishop, Elizabeth. *Complete Poems 1927 -1979.* New York: Farrar Straus Giroux, 1983.

Borges, Jorge Luis. *Labyrinths.* New York: New Directions, 1962.

Bowen, Elizabeth. *Ivy Gripped the Steps and Other Stories.* New York: Knopf, 1946.

Bowles, Paul. *The Sheltering Sky.* New York: John Lehmann, 1949.

Brande, Dorothea. *Becoming a Writer.* New York: Harcourt Brace, 1934.

Breton, André. *Nadja.* New York: Grove Press, 1994.

Brillat-Savarin, Jean Anthelme. *The Physiology of Taste.* New York: Vintage, 2011.

Brine, Duncan. *The Literary Garden.* New York: Berkley Trade, 2002.

Brontë, Charlotte. *Villette.* New York: Bantam, 1986.

Brontë, Emily. *Wuthering Heights.* New York: Dover, 1996.

Burke, Edmund. *Treatise on the Sublime and the Beautiful.* London: Oxford World Classics, 2008.

Butler, Robert Olen. *Had a Good Time.* New York: Grove Press, 2005.

Butts, Mary. *The Journal of Mary Butts.* New Haven: Yale University Press, 2002.

Calvino, Italo. *Invisible Cities.* New York: Harcourt Brace Jovanovich, 1978.

Cameron, Julia. *The Artist's Way.* New York: Tarcher/Putnam, 1992.

Cameron, Julia. *The Right to Write: An Invitation into the Writing Life.* New York: Tarcher, 1999.

Campbell, Joseph. *The Hero with a Thousand Faces.* Princeton: Bollingen Books, 1949.

Castaneda, Carlos. *The Art of Dreaming.* New York: William Morrow, 2003.

Chatwin, Bruce. *In Patagonia.* New York: Penguin, 2003.

Coelho, Paulo. *The Pilgrimage.* New York: Harper, 2008.

Coleridge, Samuel Taylor. *Selected Poetry and Prose.* New York: Penguin Poetry Library, 1985.

Cooper, Betty. *Mapping Manhattan.* New York: Harry Abrams, 2013.

Corbin, Henry. *Spiritual Body and Celestial Earth.* Princeton: Princeton University Press, 1989.

Dante Alighieri. *The Inferno.* New York: Signet, 2009.

David-Neel, Alexandra. *My Journey to Lhassa.* New York: Harper, 2005.

Daumal, René. *Mount Analogue.* New York: Overlook, 2004.

De Botton, Alain. *The Art of Travel.* New York: Pantheon, 2002.

Debord, Guy, *The Society of the Spectacle.* London: Rebel Press-Aim, 1977.

De Maistre, Xavier. *Journey Around My Room.* London: William Smith, 1845.

Dillard, Annie. *Pilgrim at Tinker Creek.* New York: Harper Perennial, 2007.

Durrell, Lawrence. *The Alexandria Quartet.* London: Faber, 1982.

Durrell, Lawrence. *Prospero's Cell.* London: Faber, 1962.

Durrell, Lawrence. *The Spirit of Place.* London: Faber, 1969.

Eco, Umberto. *Six Walks in the Fictional Woods.* Harvard University Press, 1997.

Eliade, Mircea. *The Sacred and Profane.* New York: Harcourt Brace, 1959.

Eliot, T.S. *Selected Prose.* New York: Harcourt Brace, 1975.

Emerson, Ralph Waldo. *Essays and Lectures.* New York: New American Library, 1983.

Epel, Naomi. *Writers Dreaming.* New York: Clarkston Potter, 1994.

Evans-Wentz, Walter. *The Fairy Faith in Celtic Countries.* New York: Citadel, 2003.

Fisher, M.F.K. *The Art of Eating.* New York: Houghton Mifflin, 2004.

Galland, China. *Longing for Darkness.* New York: Penguin, 2007.

Gardner, John. *The Art of Fiction.* New York: Knopf, 1984.

Gass, William. *In the Heart of the Heart of the Country and Other Stories.* New York: Harper and Row, 1968.

Goldberg, Natalie. *Writing Down the Bones.* Boston: Shambala, 2010.

Graves, Robert. *The White Goddess.* London: Faber and Faber, 1961.

Gray, Martin. *Sacred Earth: Places of Peace and Power.* New York: Sterling Publishers, 2007.

Gray, Martin. *Sacred Life: Coins of the Natural World.* Sedona: Magic Planet Productions, 2012.

Greene, Jeffrey. *The Golden Bristled Boar.* Charlottesville, VA: Univeristy of Virginia Press, 2011.

Hampl, Patricia. *Tell Me True: Memoir, History, and Writing a Life.* New York: Borealis, 2011.

Heat-Moon, William Least. *PrairyErth.* New York: Houghton Mifflin, 1999.

Heat-Moon, William Least. *Blue Highways.* New York: Little Brown, 1999.

Hiss, Tony. *Deep Travel.* New York: Knopf, 2010.

Hogan, Linda. *Dwellings.* New York: Simon and Schuster, 1995.

Hughes, Elaine Farris. *Writing from the Inner Self.* New York: Harper, 1992.

Johnson, Alexandra. *Leaving a Trace.* New York: Back Bay Books, 2002.

Jong, Erica. *Fruits and Vegetables.* New York: Holt, 1971.

Jung, C.G. *Memories, Dreams, and Reflections.* New York: Vintage, 1965.

Justice, Donald. *New and Selected Poems.* New York: Knopf, 1997.

Kennedy, Thomas E. *Kerrigan's Copenhagen.* Galway: Wynkin deWorde, 2002.

Kennedy, Thomas E. *Kerrigan in Copenhagen.* New York: Bloomsbury, 2013.

King, Stephen. *On Writing.* New York: Scribner, 2010.

Lappin, Linda. *The Etruscan.* Galway: Wynkin de Worde, 2004.

Lappin, Linda *Katherine's Wish.* Eugene: Wordcraft of Oregon, 2008.

Lappin, Linda *Signatures in Stone.* New York: Pleasure Boat Studio, 2013.

Lawrence, D.H. *Classical Studies in American Literature.* Cambridge: Cambridge University Press, 2003.

Lawrence, D. H. *Sea and Sardinia.* Cambridge: Cambridge University Press, 1997.

Lawrence, D.H. *Sketches of Etruscan Places and other Italian Essays,* Cambridge: Cambridge University Press, 2002.

Le Blanc, Barbara. *Postcards of Acadie.* Kentville, Nova Scotia: Gaspereau Press, 2003.

Mansfield, Katherine. *Selected Letters and Journals.* London: Penguin, 1977.

May, Adrian. *Myth and Creative Writing.* London: Pearson, 2011.

Menozzi, Wallis Wilde. *Mother Tongue.* New York: North Point Press, 2003.

Menozzi, Wallis Wilde. *The Other Side of the Tiber.* New York: Farrar Strauss Giroux, 2013.

Montague, John. *The Rough Field.* Winston-Salem: Wake Forest University Press, 1972.

Munro, Alice. *Selected Stories.* New York: Vintage, 1996.

Neruda, Pablo. *Selected Poems.* New York: Grove Press, 1971.

Napias, Jean-Christophe. *Quiet Corners of Paris.* New York: The Little Bookroom, 2007.

Pamuk, Orhan. *The New Life.* New York: Vintage, 1998.

Pearson Mike and Michael Shanks. *Theatre/Archaeology.* New York: Routledge, 2001.

Perec, Georges. *An Attempt at Exhausting a Place in Paris.* Adelaide: Wakefield Press, 2010.

Ponge, Francis. *The Voice of Things.* New York: McGraw Hill, 1974.

Potteiger Matthew and Purinton Jamie, *Landscape Narratives.* New York: Wiley and Sons, 1998.

Proulx, Annie. *Postcards.* New York: Scribner, 1994.

Proust, Marcel. *Swann's Way.* New York: Holt, 1922.

Ruskin, John. *The Stones of Venice.* New York: Perseus, 2003.

Salinger, J.D. *The Catcher in the Rye.* New York: Little Brown and Co., 1991.

Sarton. May. *Collected Poems.* New York: Norton, 1993.

Slawson, David. *Secret Teachings in the Art of Japanese Gardens.* New York: Kodansha America. 2013.

Snyder, Gary. *Mountains and Rivers Without End.* New York: Counterpoint, 2008.

Snyder, Gary. *The Practice of the Wild.* New York: Counterpoint, 2010.

Spalding, Lavinia. *Writing Away.* Palo Alto: Travelers' Tales, 2009.

Spiegelman, Willard. *How Poets See the World.* New York: Oxford University Press, 2007.

Thoreau, Henry David. *Walden and Other Writings.* New York: Bantam, 1983.

Tiberghien, Susan M. *One Year to a Writing Life.* New York: Marlowe, 2007.

Tiberghien, Susan M. *Looking for Gold.* Einsiedeln, Switzerland: Daimon Verlag, 1997.

Travers, P.L. *What the Bee Knows.* New York: Codhill, 1989.

Wharton, Edith. *Italian Villas and Their Gardens.* New York: Becker Press, 2013.

White, Edmund. *The Flâneur.* New York: Bloomsbury, 2001.

Wordsworth, William. *The Collected Poems.* New York: Wordsworth Poetry Library. 1998.

Woolf, Virginia. *Essays Vol. 1: 1904–1912.*New York: Mariner Books, 1989.

Linda Lappin

Woolf, Virginia. *Essays Vol.2: 1912–1918.* New York: Mariner Books, 1991.
Woolf, Virginia. *Moments of Being.* New York: Mariner Books, 1985.
Wortsman, Peter. *Ghost Dance in Berlin.* Palo Alto: Travelers' Tales, 2013.
Wright, Charles. *Appalachia.* New York: Farrar, Strauss, Giroux, 1999.
Yeats, W.B. *A Vision.* New York: Collier Books, 1966.
Yeats, W.B. *Selected Poems.* New York: Scribner, 1996.

About the Author

Linda Lappin is an American poet, novelist, and travel writer. She has published three novels, *The Etruscan, Katherine's Wish,* and *Signatures in Stone: A Bomarzo Mystery,* which won the 2014 Daphne Du Maurier Award for Mystery and Suspense Writing. She holds an MFA from the University of Iowa Writers Workshop.